JOHN

HAYDN
Piano Sonatas

BBC MUSIC GUIDES

ARIEL MUSIC
BBC PUBLICATIONS

Published by BBC Publications
A division of BBC Enterprises Ltd
35 Marylebone High Street, London W1M 4AA

ISBN 0 563 20481 8

First published 1986

Typeset in 10/11 pt Garamond by Phoenix Photosetting, Chatham
Printed in England by Mackays of Chatham Ltd

Contents

Introduction

Haydn's keyboard sonatas were composed throughout his career from the earliest days until his second visit to London in 1794/95, when he was 62, so although they do not represent the music of his last decade they do show his enormous development as a composer up to that period. They do so, perhaps, neither so clearly nor on so large a scale as the symphonies and string quartets, the other genres in which he made his most consistent contribution to the repertoire, but vividly enough, often illuminating aspects of his changing style not so nearly touched on in the other works. It is often said that the mark of a really fine composer is that his ideas stem from the medium in which he or she is working and that therefore a composer will write slightly different music stylistically for orchestra than for string quartet, solo keyboard, or chorus. No writer more successfully upholds this theory than Haydn, whose works are almost always perfectly attuned to their medium and would almost invariably lose something of their essence if transferred to another setting. (The validity of *The Seven Last Words*, which exists in several versions from chorus and orchestra to string quartet and even, in an arrangement not written by but approved by Haydn, for keyboard, hardly affects this judgement, since that work is of its very nature utterly different to anything else he wrote.)

Occasionally in the course of this study I refer to the shameful neglect of Haydn's sonatas, a neglect I find it difficult to understand. There can hardly be another such corpus of outstanding and fascinating works by one of the great masters so wilfully ignored by performers, nor one so frequently misunderstood. My object in this Guide, therefore, has been to try and give precisely a guide to the music, a description of each work in an attempt to place it in its context, both in terms of Haydn's output and of the contemporary world where this seems appropriate. There are some topics which seem beyond the scope of such a brief survey – the discussion of instruments used is one, though it is touched on a few times. I should, however, make clear my own strong predilection for performance of the works on the modern piano, since only then, I feel, do we hear the music in the round, so to speak, with an awareness both of the traditions from which it sprang and those which it was helping to establish, even of those to which it was leading the way: more than any other major composer, Haydn documents in his keyboard works the change from earlier instruments to the piano. To place these works under a glass case by performing them on roughly contemporaneous

7

instruments (or modern remakes) is fascinating, often revealing, but for me it tends to restrict the music's significance by anchoring it too firmly to its period. I am aware of other arguments, and can often see their justice, but I regard this point as of paramount importance. I hope those who disagree with me will nevertheless find something of interest in these pages.

Another associated topic that is too large to be dealt with here is that of the sources of the sonata and sonata form. During the course of this Guide, reference is made whenever apt to traditions both past and present relating to these works. In this way, I hope to have built up a picture of the stylistic context of the sonatas, relating to them as individual pieces. For proper descriptions of the basic background to the sonata as a Classical phenomenon the reader must look elsewhere – Denis Matthews's BBC Music Guide to the *Beethoven Piano Sonatas* (1967) has a useful introduction in this regard, and Rosemary Hughes's Guide to the *Haydn String Quartets* (1966) touches invaluably on questions of sonata form. For deeper study, William S. Newman's tome *The Sonata in the Classic Era* (University of North Carolina Press, 1963) is statutory reading. In this Guide I refer several times to the massive five-volume work by H. C. Robbins Landon *Haydn: Chronicle and Works*, published during the 1970s by Thames and Hudson in the following volumes: (i) *The Early Years 1732–65*, (ii) *Haydn at Eszterháza 1766–90*, (iii) *Haydn in England 1791–95*, (iv) *The Years of 'The Creation', 1796–1800*, and (v) *The Late Years, 1801–09*. This wonderful work is indispensable for those who want to investigate the minutiae of Haydn's life and works, and is the summation of Robbins Landon's efforts on behalf of his beloved composer.

The question of the numbering of the sonatas is a vexed one. When Christa Landon's edition appeared in the 1960s, published in the *Wiener Urtext Edition* by Universal Edition, they became at once the finest available edition, and the most invaluable. Hitherto, the numbering (for 52 sonatas) given in the catalogue by Anthony van Hoboken, published in 1957 by Schott & Co., had been used as the complete listing. It was taken from the Breitkopf und Härtel edition published in 1918, edited by Carl Päsler and referred to hereafter as Päsler/Hoboken. Christa Landon's edition lists 62 sonatas, with some changes to the actual contents of the catalogue as well as the order, and is based on the many discoveries made since Päsler produced his chronology and Hoboken adopted it. The numberings in this Guide are, therefore, prefaced by the letter L denoting the Christa Landon edition, and I have placed the Päsler/Hoboken numbers prefaced by 'Hob.' in brackets after them. In Hoboken's catalogue, the sonatas form category XVI (just as the symphonies are group I, for instance). I have always felt that a designation such as 'Sonata in G minor, XVI/44' is more daunting than informative as far as audiences are concerned, and look forward to the day when 'Sonata in G minor, L. 32' is as commonplace a title as 'Sonata in A minor, K. 310' is for Mozart.

Few composers have lived through a period of such monumental musical upheaval as Haydn, at any rate until the past century. As a young man, brought up in the traditions of church and entertainment music of the High Baroque with a strong archaic element (the church music of Palestrina was still a vital, living part of the liturgical world in which he spent his youth), he saw music move gradually through a period of greater expressiveness and subjectivity to the great glories of the Viennese Classical tradition, and he died on the threshold of Romanticism. To have been able to respond with such unfailing intelligence and insight to this metamorphosis is an enormous achievement — one has only to think of the way Haydn learnt, very late in life, from the impact of Handel's oratorios and found the inspiration not merely to attempt the same medium but also to produce two of its greatest masterworks, *The Creation* and *The Seasons*, without losing one iota of his own distinctive musical personality. It is a tribute to his strength of character and clarity of vision. The sonatas may, on the whole, be lesser works, but they reflect many fascinating aspects of his progress, and include a far greater number of first-class works than seems generally realised. They reflect, too, the essential humanity of their composer, expressed in however modest a format. Their riches, both technical and expressive, are inexhaustible.

The Early Sonatas: (i) L. 1–12

One of the great difficulties in assessing the earliest sonatas, and one that remains with some of the later works, is the absence of properly authenticated sources. The first three in Christa Landon's edition, along with No. 13, were advertised in 1766 as being available in manuscript copies from Breitkopf, but movements from early sonatas also occur in some of the early piano trios (and in one case a baryton trio). That the finale of No. 4 appears also as the first movement of No. 5 supports H. C. Robbins Landon's proposal (in Vol. 1 of *Chronicle and Works*) that some individual movements of early sonatas and trios 'may have originated as single movements, "lessons", for pupils and have been put together as sonatas or trios, sometimes by Haydn, sometimes by friends, pupils, or, indeed, the clever Viennese copyists . . . the composer may have allowed them a certain artistic licence in preparing such works for commercial purposes.' Certainly the nature of many of these early movements suggests a pedagogic purpose – they are sometimes the very model of charming teaching pieces. Indeed, Feder, in his edition (published by Henle), groups the first 18 sonatas in two categories, 'Nine small early sonatas' (i.e. works intended for students or amateurs) and 'Nine early sonatas' (works written for more professional performers). The former group comprises Landon Nos. 10, 2, 1, 3, 6, 4, 7, 14 and 9, and the latter are Landon 8, 12, 15, 16, 13, 11, 17, 18 and the E flat work, Hoboken XVI: 16, omitted from the Christa Landon edition. At the same time, primitive though they may be in their handling of structure and harmonic motion, they do indicate Haydn's relationship to his contemporaries and, in embryo, some of the elements that were later to develop so strikingly in his sonatas.

The Sonata No. 1 in G (Hob. 8) is an example of several characteristic types of movement at this period. It is unusual in having four movements (only No. 13, also in the 'open-air' key of G, does this too), and the first is a genuine, if minute, sonata form. The opening theme, delightfully sturdy and forthright, contains several elements suitable for varied development, notably the dotted rhythm and simple, arpeggiated nature of the first bar (it was the Mannheim symphonists who developed this style of creating an opening theme from the notes of the common chord) and the triplet tag in bars 3–4 – the bass merely sketches in the essential tonal and harmonic scheme.

There is no transition before the second subject proceeds (Ex. 1(a) opposite, bar 8), typically giving what might otherwise seem a purely

Ex. 1(a)

Ex. 1(b)

Ex. 1(c)

harmonic bass line a more melodic slant through its contrast with the off-beat, repeated notes in the right hand. The brief ten-bar development section concerns itself largely with the off-beat notes from the second subject and the triplet tag from the first, with an occasional dotted rhythm to remind us of the first bar and an interesting inversion of the scalic phrase from the codetta of the exposition (Exx. 1(b) and 1(c)). It is perhaps a shade unfortunate that, in the recapitulation, the almost exact repetition of the first subject leads to a clumsy reversion to the tonic key for the second, but nevertheless this elegant little piece, for all its simplicity, contains some of the seeds of Haydn's organic thinking.

His debt to composers such as Wagenseil, J. G. Reutter, jr, and Galuppi is explored in Robbins Landon's *Chronicle and Works*, Vol. 1, and would require too much detail to go into here. Suffice it to mention one aspect of his technique that owes much to Wagenseil – the deliberate use of the elements of ornamentation as a distinct part of the melodic style. In Ex. 1(a), the triplet tag in bars 3–4 is simply a turn, but written-out carefully to reveal its role as an essential part of the melodic thought. This *Allegro* also shows the essentially motivic nature of Haydn's technique. The Menuet which follows (without trio section) inaugurates that long series of such movements in which his minuet style developed in two different directions: one leading to the fast scherzo that Beethoven used to be credited with inventing, and the other retaining the poised minuet manner but enriching, varying, and elaborating it in different ways. This example is straightforward, but in its first four bars one can note Haydn's typical use of rests in the melodic line (the bass serving the purpose of both implying the full harmonies and keeping the music moving forwards), the ornamental nature of the right-hand phrase in bar 2, and his beloved triplet figure in bar 3:

Ex. 2

At the start of the second section of this bipartite movement, there is a surprising and delightful modulation to A minor, something repeated even more expressively at the start of the third movement's second section. The first half of this lyrical *Andante* (in G, like all the movements) is simpler and more melodic, a genuine 'tune' as opposed to a collection of motifs, above a slightly Baroque-sounding 'walking bass' harking back to continuo traditions, but the second half is less sustained melodically and more developmental. The work is rounded off by a breezy *Allegro* in 3/8 time, well over half of which lies entirely above middle C, an early example of Haydn's willingness to exploit particular keyboard registers.

The three-movement Sonata No. 2 in C (Hob. 7) also has some points of interest. The opening *Allegro moderato*, initiated by three decisive chords moving outwards, is a mere 23 bars long (the first movement of No. 1 is 44 bars), but this time the Menuet, again placed second, does have a trio section. While the Menuet itself is not particularly notable save for its juxtaposition of a lyrical four bars with a more military phrase, the trio is significant. In C minor, though with a key signature of only two flats, it has a new expressiveness, even a hint of pathos, emphasised by the darker colouring produced by the use of scalic thirds – the right hand's drooping phrases in thirds are especially sensitive, and there are touches of greater chromaticism (notably at the beginning of the second half, where Haydn subtly implies that major/minor ambiguity which fascinates tonal composers even today). The final *Allegro*, in 3/8, is not unlike that of the preceding work, though more extensive and a touch more virtuosic – of particular note is a three-bar phrase of left-hand broken octaves moving upwards unaccompanied (rather like an accompaniment to a missing tune). The flexibility of the phrase-structure is especially marked in the opening theme, which has two three-bar phrases, and the opening of the second section (in itself a kind of mild development), which starts with two six-bar phrases each made up of two plus four.

The splendid Sonata No. 3 in F (Hob. 9) again has three movements, and, though not markedly larger in scale than its predecessor, has more authority, even a touch of imperious grandeur. This is most marked in the opening *Allegro*, with its greater use of bass octaves and a wider bass range. Formally, the exposition is an early example of a typical Haydn sonata-exposition structure: opening theme, 'expansion section' gradually establishing the dominant key, and closing section in the dominant. This modestly-proportioned but impressive piece is well sustained, and something of the same quality informs the succeeding Menuet and trio. Here it is the Menuet which, though simple and straightforward, has a four-bar minor-key section adding sensitivity to the music, while the B flat major trio, a shade more lyrical, shows a keen awareness of the textural richness achieved by acutely-judged spacings. Of much importance is the title of the deft, witty finale, an *Allegro* marked *scherzo*. This title, which came to mean such different things as the later Haydn and Beethoven symphonic movements and the Chopin piano pieces, derives from such sources as Monteverdi's *Scherzi Musicale* (Musical Jokes) and the German word *Scherz* ('joke'). Here, as elsewhere, Haydn gives us a scherzo in duple metre – there is as yet no sign of his development of the minuet towards this type of characterisation. It is short and delightful – the wit is emphasised if the performer, instead of finishing loudly, plays the final phrase *piano* and rather delicately, as if to catch the listener by surprise.

That Sonatas 4 and 5 have a movement in common has already been noted. No. 4 in G was omitted by Päsler (in Hoboken it appears as XVI/G1), but of the two it is the more convincing as an entity. Originally entitled Divertimento, like so many of the early sonatas, it has a generously-sized opening *Allegro*. The sprightly first theme of seven bars is followed by a related five-bar phrase modulating to the dominant for the second subject, clearly a variant of the first:

Ex. 3(a)

Ex. 3(b)

The movement lasts 80 bars, and is expanded by a development section making extensive use of fairly obvious sequences, and by a brief passage in which the downward scale of the up-beat in Ex. 3 is transferred to the left hand and treated sequentially. The Menuet and trio are stately, so much so that they have a faintly comic air, enhanced in the Menuet by some bassoon-like broken octaves in the left hand. The C major trio is more sparse, and full of rests, so that the ornamentation (which the player might be expected to vary on repeats) assumes an extra importance as a vital melodic element. The finale is a short, bright 3/8 *Presto* which is surely another scherzo in character – this too has a trio (in G minor), the main G major part being then repeated. The concluding phrases of the first half of the trio sections of the second and third movements are, given the difference in tonality and mood, virtually the same.

It is the finale of this sonata which opens Sonata No. 5 (Hob. 11), though it makes far less sense as a first movement. In this position it even seems less charming, and is far outweighed by the succeeding *Andante* (63 bars long) in G minor. This exquisitely simple piece uses sequences and left-hand suspensions to poignant effect, and though it looks on paper rather four-square and plodding, in performance it can become imbued with an expansive spirit of sad reflection. As if to banish

this mood, the G major Menuet begins brusquely and determinedly with a tune in octaves of distinctly peasant-dance character. It is the B minor trio that is particularly noteworthy, however, for its exceptional flexibility of phrase-lengths. The first section comprises seven bars plus four – the music is given an added fluidity by the first full bar effectively acting as an up-beat to the second. This kind of dislocation runs throughout the trio, and it is a pity that these two fascinating movements should be preceded by one so clearly in the wrong context.

Like this work, the Sonata No. 6 in C (Hob. 10) was advertised as available in manuscript copies from Breitkopf in 1767, and it is a much more satisfying piece as a whole, rich in significant detail despite its simplicity. There is a clear relationship between the opening phrases of each movement, rising from C to G:

Ex. 4(a)

Ex. 4(b)   **Ex. 4(c)**

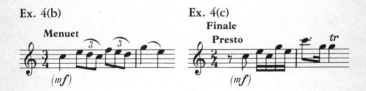

(In passing, it might be noted that the incipit to the finale is very similar to that of the finale of Sonata No. 3 in F.) The first movement, *Moderato*, is largely monothematic, mainly dominated by the rhythm ♫♫♫ from bar 1 (Ex. 4(a) above). This forms both first and, with some mild development, second subjects, and the little tag following the former recurs and is extended to lead to the codetta material. The rhythmic motif also dominates the development, though the tag-figure is extended through a seven-bar phrase to lead to the recapitulation. This, and the five-bar phrases of the codetta and coda, are the only disruptions of the otherwise regular four-bar phrasing, but the music never seems stultified – its freshness and vigour is aided not only by the ebullience of the material but also by the sparkling trills which frequently colour it.

The graceful Menuet is both lyrical and sturdy, almost entirely in four-bar groups save for the six-bar phrase which, by extending the format, gives extra emphasis to the close. The C minor trio is expressive, full of Baroque-like suspensions and sequences:

Ex. 5

In the second half, Haydn uses to great effect a degree of syncopation, a device common at that time to suggest a kind of written-out rubato. The high-spirited, virtuosic finale has four main ideas: the opening (see Ex. 4(c) above), a more self-contained circling phrase in the dominant giving rise to some Handelian sequences, a gentler series of G minor two-note phrases in thirds, and a brilliantly flourishing series of triplets outlining a descending G major arpeggio. The feeling of the movement is that of a sonata form, with a development section based mainly on a figuration later to become very familiar – Georg Feder has pointed out the resemblance between part of this and part of the next sonata:

Ex. 6(a)

Ex. 6(b)

'Both passages are joined together not only by the same figuration, the same rhythm, the same tempo, but also by a very similar modulation with similar steps in the bass. In each piece they have even the same function: a temporary modulation in the development section of the finale shortly before the return to the recapitulation. Nevertheless one is not a slavish imitation of the other.[1] For the recapitulation, all four main ideas are now in the tonic, with the scintillating triplets ascending to add an extra note of exuberance.

In the Preface to her edition, Christa Landon justified her inclusion of Sonata No. 7 in D among the sonatas, despite its listing in Hoboken under *Klavierstücke* (group XVII) as D1, because its three movements make it seem closer to the sonata than to the *Klavierstücke*. It is hardly an imposing work, and seems rather incomplete (the central Menuet, for instance, lacks a trio), but the outer movements have some interest. The first, *Moderato*, is a theme and three variations, with an unvaried bass line. Though simple, the variations are not unresourceful in their handling of the thematic material, and this does after all mark the first appearance in the sonatas (assuming we accept the new chronology) of a form that became an essential part of Haydn's structural armoury. It gives the performer an excellent opportunity to indulge in some varied and lyrical ornamentation for the repeats. The finale, already referred to (Ex. 6(b) above), is brief and lively – the first theme commences with unison octaves stating the notes of an upward D major chord, a typical Mannheim device not unlike their famous 'rockets'. The codetta and coda give a momentary nod in the direction of Domenico Scarlatti, something to become familiar in Haydn's keyboard style. It is also worth noting, again in the finale, that for a few bars the left-hand part lies higher than the right-hand – it was the crossed-hands passage in Sonata No. 59 that was to give Marianne von Genzinger such difficulty.

Several authorities have cast serious doubts on the provenance of Sonata No. 8 in A (Hob. 5), the first keyboard composition made generally available under Haydn's name. Christa Landon says: 'The authenticity of Sonata No. 8, advertised by Breitkopf in 1763, is most doubtful. The primitive setting with its succession of unrelated phrases and the puerile modulations does not suggest Haydn's authorship. . . . Although this sonata belongs to those works summarily acknowledged by Haydn in 1803, when going through the thematic lists for the *Oeuvres complettes* . . . it can scarcely have been possible for the ageing Haydn to recall each and every composition of such an early date.' Charles Rosen, in his book *Sonata Forms*, puts it even more bluntly: 'the silly Sonata in A major . . . almost certainly not by Haydn.' It would be

1 In *Studies in Eighteenth-Century Music*, ed. Robbins Landon and Chapman (London, 1970).

hubris to argue with these authorities, and certainly these strictures apply to the opening *Allegro* – among other things, one is aware that the Alberti bass appears occasionally, something not hitherto encountered in these works and unusual even in Haydn's later ones (often, indeed, a bad sign when it does occur). There are extraordinarily dull repetitions of uninteresting phrases, while the introduction into the development of two gratuitous ideas not heard in the exposition seems unrelated to anything therein. But there are some interesting things, too, such as a flexible metrical structure in which motifs overlap and lead rapidly from one to another. The second subject, preceded by a huge expansion section, is given the minor-key signature and is separated from the surrounding major-key material by emphatic rests. The order of events in the second half is unusual – the opening theme (of a distinctly Italianate *galant* style, something normal in early Haydn) recurring only in the dominant at the start of the development and being omitted altogether from the recapitulation. In the latter the tonic, in root position, is only reached fully for the second subject, in the tonic minor, and only after material from what might loosely be termed the first subject group has already been heard. If this work is actually by Haydn, then it marks an early instance of his love of dovetailing or developing the material during the recapitulation, and of changing the order of its reappearance during it. Both the Mannheim composers and Domenico Scarlatti were fond of arriving back at the tonic key in the manner adopted in this movement.

The Menuet and trio, both extremely simple, are less interesting – there is a plodding gait about them that precludes Haydn's characteristic flow and leads one to feel that if it were really by him he would have opened out the texture a little with some rests, in the use of which he was a master from the start. The finale, a *Presto* in 3/8, is the best movement – as in the *Allegro*, there are some clumsy rhythmic phrasings and modulations, but the main theme is lively (again the music is rather Italianate) and the stomping peasant-dance nature of the codetta material is delightful.

There are no doubts about the genuineness of Sonata No. 9 in D (Hob. 4). The first of the two movements, *Moderato*, is marvellously lyrical – there is a sense of a new expansiveness about the writing, sustained throughout from the opening seven-bar phrase.

Some toccata figuration in D major follows, turned into a melodic flow by the moderate pace and by its relationship every half bar with the second half of bar 3 (Ex. 7, right hand) – when the dominant is reached,

Ex. 7

it is for the codetta material, based on flowing triplets. There seems an ambiguity about whether there is a 'real' second subject or not – if there is, it is either in the 'wrong' key (the tonic) or the 'wrong' place (the codetta). But it is merely that the form is tripartite: first subject, expansion section leading to the dominant, closing section (or codetta) in the dominant. The development simply contrasts the opening couple of bars with the lyrical toccata material twice (the appearance of a series of lovely modulations starting with the main theme in B minor is a particularly beautiful moment) – the recapitulation is straightforward. This serene movement is followed by a Menuet and trio notable mainly for the plain 'two-part-invention' style of the latter.

If Sonata No. 8 is unauthentic, then No. 10 in C (Hob. 1) marks the first significant incursion of the Alberti bass into the sonatas, and it serves here the purpose that it usually serves with Haydn, that of artificially maintaining the music's momentum. Truth to tell, the opening *Allegro* has always seemed to me singularly dull, despite the promising vigour of the first theme, another note-by-note statement of the common chord – the development strangely anticipates that in Mozart's little C major Sonata, K. 545. Nor is the Menuet and trio especially noteworthy, save for some expressive syncopations in the C minor trio. It is in the mellifluous central *Adagio* that most interest lies. This is a characteristic arioso type, to be found in numerous works by such contemporaries as Wagenseil and Reutter, a continuous stream of elegant triplets over a simple bass, pulsating gently. There is a more sophisticated, more touching example in G minor in the Sonata No. 13 discussed later. A different arioso style is on display in the next sonata, No. 11 in B flat (Hob. 2), a far more consistent work and perhaps the most impressive so far – certainly it is the most ambitious.

In the slow movement of this fine work, Haydn sets out before us a lengthy, poignant melody whose throbbing accompaniment emphasises its intense feeling. With the dramatic and richly scored chord in bar 7 Haydn indicates his awareness of newly expanded tonal areas:

Ex. 8

This powerful cadence would suggest, in a conventional sonata scheme, that we have arrived at the point for the second subject, the dominant major. Instead of maintaining the key to which he has moved, however, Haydn immediately switches with memorable effect to B flat major (the relative major) and embarks on a lovely series of, first, upward-wreathing scales and, then, chains of curling syncopations which unsettle the metre to the extent of suggesting a momentary 6/8 pulse in the basic 3/4 context. Both the areas of technical resourcefulness and expressiveness are vastly extended from those shown in previous works, and in the 'development' Haydn indulges in something equally novel for him, a few bars of genuine, chromatic two-part counterpoint:

Ex. 9

The splendid first movement (*Moderato*) is no less rich in incident or material. The main theme combines Haydn's favourite type of fanfare-like exploration of the common chord with his equally beloved use of ornamental triplets as an essential part of the melody line:

Ex. 10

Once this springy manner has been established, it is maintained to the end of the largest movement thus far (148 bars), in which the range of the keyboard is handled with flexibility, rhythmic interest sustained throughout, and sequential patterns used with freedom and assurance. Several Scarlattian touches add to the music's vivacity. The sonata ends with a Menuet and trio of larger proportions than hitherto, the former resuming something of the lively bounce of the *Moderato* in a more relaxed fashion, the trio a most beautiful piece in B flat minor (an indication that Haydn, like so many of his contemporaries, was interested in some uncommon keys), notable once again for its delicate handling of off-beat notes and suspensions in the right hand.

The neglect of this work, which one would expect to attract pianists seeking something intimate yet vivacious, is inexplicable – it stands out among the early works for its approach to a more symphonic style, admittedly in a still modest way. No. 12 in A (Hob. 12 – the only work given the same number by both Päsler/Hoboken and Christa Landon) is not nearly so forward-looking or large-scale. In some respects it is even backward-looking, though the new spaciousness is still in evidence. The idyllic first movement, *Andante*, is an almost continuous flow of triplets derived from a theme of vocal elegance (it is comparatively rare for Haydn's themes, normally so instrumental in inspiration, to have a vocal character). Though the writing is mature, the tonality remains centred on tonic and dominant keys, even in the development section, reminding one of the extreme simplicity of the earliest sonatas, and the maintenance of one texture throughout recalls the style of the Baroque suite. Placed second, the Menuet and trio are radically different from each other, with a conventional Menuet contrasting a trio employing right-hand syncopations above a steadily moving bass part that, at the start, is almost reminiscent of Purcell:

Ex. 11

The finale is a sprightly *Allegro molto* in 3/8, using melodic material of the utmost simplicity (the main theme opens, one note per bar, with the first four notes of the A major scale, with an inverted mordent on each one) and a good deal of Alberti bass – but it is not too long to outstay its welcome, and the phrase-lengths are cunningly balanced.

The Early Sonatas: (ii) L. 13–30

The danger, when performing, studying, or listening to Haydn's sonatas in chronological order, is that in the case of the first 16 or so, the similarities between them become more noticeable and their individual characters less marked than if they are viewed in isolation or with some of the later ones. It is therefore easy to overlook the very real qualities of such works as No. 11, and there are others among those already discussed which repay close and sympathetic attention. Without wishing to overstate the case, however, I have no doubt that No. 13 in G (Hob. 6) marks an important move forward in Haydn's development. It is a four-movement work, originally titled *Partita per il Clavicembalo Solo* and certainly written before 1760 (possibly as early as 1755). Its brevity is in the tradition of the earlier works but it is more adventurous in its wealth of material and imaginative in its handling of rhythm and texture. The *Allegro*'s opening theme gives an idea of Haydn's new-found sense of freedom, particularly in the bass line, a harmonic/tonal underpinning and yet a melodic line in its own right:

Ex. 12

This example surely conveys the fine sweep of the first phrase – it cannot, however, indicate the variety contained within this movement, typified by the fact that with the next phrase Haydn already starts to develop his material. He introduces new features, such as dotted rhythms and flowing triplets, as well as extending the typical tag *x* with which he makes great play in both halves of the movement. At the up-beat to bar 5, having reached the dominant, he embarks on what is technically a second subject, an open-air march tune in dotted rhythms typical of the divertimenti of the period. From the conventional sonata-form point of view this hardly justifies the title 'second subject' – for one thing, it occurs too early in the scheme to carry its full structural weight. This is simply not a straightforward sonata movement – it is, rather, a beautifully balanced set of motifs often closely inter-related and having its own logic, with much overlapping of sections. In the second half, the opening theme is heard at the start, this time in D major, but disappears thereafter — instead of development/recapitulation, this part consists in effect of a recapitulation which is at the same time development or even variation. Tonally, this *Allegro* is notable for its flexibility, with exploration of a wide range of keys closely related to G major and, in the codetta sections, a subtle and charming use of minor inflections. It makes a lovely and entertaining movement, far more richly worked than its apparent spontaneity might suggest.

The Minuet and trio are less striking, though the Minuet is a particularly fine example of its kind, simple but stately, with a little more variety of texture than hitherto, and the trio, in G minor, is chromatic and touchingly expressive. The *Adagio* which follows is a miracle of sensitivity, a Bachian arioso of great lyrical beauty based on flowing triplets in a manner having much in common with the contemporary slow movement style:

Ex. 13

This serene and poignant *Adagio* contains two points at which it reaches a fermata with a pause, when the performer is clearly expected to improvise some kind of brief cadenza, the first time this has occurred in the sonatas. The finale (*Allegro molto*) dispels the reflective, personal mood with an outburst of high spirits — fireworks, even. In 3/8, it has much in common formally with the first movement, including the early and decisive arrival on the dominant, but it is as a virtuoso display piece that it makes its special impact — if it was indeed written for teaching purposes, the prowess of Haydn's pupils must have increased considerably, for there is no other movement in his sonata output of quite such mercurial brilliance.

It is possible that his pupils were more adept by now, for as he became more well-known Haydn's employment became steadily more aristocratic and he began to move in more established musical circles. The Sonata No. 14 in C (Hob. 3), however, hardly suggests this – the first of the three movements, *Allegretto*, is a mild little piece, quite perky but over-reliant on the Alberti bass figuration. It bears as much relation to his better sonatas, even of this period, as do the much-maligned Clementi's sonatinas to his far greater sonatas. There is a charming but not outstanding G major *Andante*, mostly in two parts (the plainness of texture, sustained a shade too long, suggests a lack of the creative fire which marked the previous sonata), and it is only in the Menuet that anything untoward occurs. This is the first of its type in these works to start with an up-beat, one comprising, moreover, four semiquavers, a figuration which proceeds to dominate the Menuet to the almost complete exclusion of the formerly all-pervasive triplets. This might be seen as a first step along the route leading to the metamorphosis of the minuet into the scherzo. The flowing C minor trio once again has a key signature with only two flats.

On a much higher level of inspiration is Sonata No. 15 in E (Hob. 13), again in three movements. The first, *Moderato*, is especially lovely, sweetly lyrical and impregnated with a subtle variety of motifs and ideas. Unlike many of Haydn's first subjects, this one is largely scalic rather than arpeggiated, and he uses syncopations, sequences, and (towards the close of each half) delicate hints of a somewhat military dotted rhythm to add extra touches of depth to an essentially modest piece. The opening of the second half is interesting in that, having begun in the dominant with a variation of the second subject (or expansion group) material, he immediately reverts to the tonic key and an apparently straightforward recapitulation of the first part, only to veer off again with more development moving with some intensity to C sharp minor. It is a short, radiant movement, typically resourceful in its handling of form and material. The Menuet is a paradigm of Haydn's simplest minuet style, with an E minor trio of rather ominous cast, while in the finale – a stomping *Presto* reminiscent of a peasant dance – the military touches from the *Moderato* come to the fore with some splendid fanfare figures. The short development is mainly sequential (Handel comes to mind more than once), but precisely judged in length so that it makes its point without outstaying its welcome. This is another of those little works whose excellence rewards and entertains performers and listeners alike.

Sonata No. 16 in D (Hob. 14) is similar in tone, with a relaxedly lyrical *Allegro moderato*, a strong and rather more imposing Menuet and trio, and a jolly finale. The final *Allegro* is, indeed, even wittier – the military forthrightness is replaced by a humorous treatment of rests which constantly interrupt the progress of the music as if it had forgotten where it was going, and some equally delightful sideways excursions into unexpected keys for comic or expressive purposes. This is perhaps Haydn's most consistently witty movement so far. The Menuet and trio are quite impressive in their quiet determination, especially the minor-key trio. The *Allegro moderato* is exceptionally spacious and lyrical, with imaginative handling of tonality and form. Having established the tonic key with the opening theme, Haydn introduces other motifs which move the tonalities sequentially forward but never arrive at the dominant one is anticipating, nor is there a clear second subject. Instead, the first two-thirds of the movement are really one large first subject group with its own developmental aspects. A figure based on arpeggiated diminished chords (to recur, slightly varied, as the codetta material in the finale) leads us to the dominant, but instead of a new theme there are a few bars of two-part counterpoint not unlike Ex. 9 above, in the dominant minor, and then a little fanfare figure based on repeated thirds, in A major.

The next three sonatas present even more problems of text and/or authenticity than most. In the case of Nos. 17 and 18, both in E flat and both omitted in Päsler/Hoboken, manuscript copies were discovered by Feder in the former Raigern Monastery in Moravia. More recently, Carsten Hatting found another copy of No. 18, giving the composer's name as Mariano Romano Kayser (or Kaiser), about whom nothing seems to be known. Of the two works, 'Kayser's' is certainly the more assured and inventive. It opens with a lively *Allegro moderato* full of characteristic repetitions, sequences, triplets, dotted rhythms and trills, and based on a delightfully springy main theme (the way he starts the second subject group by rhythmic diminution out of the immediately preceding modulatory phrase is an inspired touch), followed by a substantial, varied Menuet with a beautifully sustained *enchaînement* of syncopations for the trio. The first movement's development, incidentally, contains a remarkable sequence of chords typical of Haydn throughout his sonata output, expressed in some Baroque figuration. A chain of seventh harmonies leads, at a rate of one chord per bar, from F minor to G, where it hovers uneasily for four bars before taking off again via F minor and, now at a rate of half-a-bar per chord, E flat, B flat (seventh), and C minor, turning suddenly to resolve firmly on G major once more. The careful judgement of the changing pace of the harmonic progressions nicely balances the sense first of travelling hopefully and then, with increasing eagerness, arriving.

If these movements are not by Haydn, then Kayser (if it is he) deserves much praise for writing them. The finale, discovered by Hatting and published by Christa Landon as an Appendix to the Editor's Report on her edition, is a sad anti-climax, unimaginative and unconvincing to a degree. No. 17, too, is a curate's egg of a work – there are excellent moments, and others which suggest that the composer's mind was elsewhere. Yet it has a number of characteristic touches and some surprising links with other Haydn works – perhaps it might be a work by one of his followers. The opening *Moderato*'s main theme is mainly a straightforward upward scale, not particularly inspired, but once again triplets and dotted rhythms play a typical part in the movement's progress, and, interestingly enough, the 'recapitulation' is considerably shortened. There are at least two ideas in this *Moderato* anticipating the A flat Sonata, No. 31, and the following *Andante*, a pleasant C minor piece opening with a theme whose first bar reminds one of the slow movement of Sonata No. 5 and, even more strongly, of the far more consistent and rewarding *Andante* of Symphony No. 37 in C. The Menuet is unremarkable save for the slight kinship with the wind dialogues of Symphony No. 22 (*The Philosopher*) in the C minor trio.

The case of No. 19 in E (also missing from Päsler/Hoboken) is different, for not only is it known to be authentic but it exists in two versions. The one published by Artaria in 1788 is now numbered 57 (Hob. 47) in F – this transposes revisions of No. 19's first two movements, placing them second and third and prefacing them with a new opening *Allegro*. The earlier version, thought to have been composed in the early 1760s, was discovered more recently in Vienna by Jens Peter Larsen – the *Adagio* is the first movement and the *Allegro* the second, with a *Tempo di Menuet* as finale. No. 57 will be considered in its place – meanwhile, as No. 19 this version has much interest. The *Adagio* is in E minor (the first of the sonatas to start in the minor), and has the rhythm of the siciliano, whose popularity was sustained through the Classical period and appeared in such works as Mozart's F major Sonata, K. 280, for the slow movement, and in the theme of the opening variations of the popular A major sonata, K. 331. This example is notable for its eloquence and decorativeness, and for a remarkably rich change of harmony near the beginning:

Ex. 14

It is in keeping with the sonata *da chiesa* influence on the sonata that the *Adagio* ends not with a full close but with a half-close on the dominant to lead to the boisterous *Allegro*. There are several other instances of such an *attacca* in the sonatas (cf. Nos. 39 and 50, both in D), and it is a device also used in the piano trios, even in some of those written in the period 1755–60 – it first occurs in the F minor trio, No. 14 in Robbins Landon's edition (Hob. XV:f1), where the first movement reaches a full close but is then marked *Sieg{ue} Minuet*. (The first example in the piano trios of a siciliano leading to the next movement after a half-close, as in this sonata, occurs in Landon No. 20 in D (Hob. XV:7), between second and third movements.) The *Allegro* itself, which begins by transforming the start of the siciliano into an ebullient major-key tune, is of fairly generous size, and though it conforms very roughly with the vague concept of 'sonata form' that is becoming established, it has at the same time a decidedly rondo-like feeling, enhanced by the fact that the 'development' starts with a substantial reference to the main theme (in the dominant) giving it the impression of a ritornello. It marks, in short, a distinct stage in the development of the hybrid sonata-rondo form. The marking for the finale, *Tempo di Menuet*, is significant, too – there is no trio, nor is one necessary, for here too the music is spacious (68 bars, with both halves repeated), with sufficient lyrical variety to make a trio superfluous – and, as so often in Haydn's sonata *da chiesa*-inspired works, a minuet makes a satisfying, dignified conclusion.

Thought to have been written during 1766/7, or perhaps even later, the B flat major Sonata No. 20 (Hob. 18) is the first in Christa Landon's edition to which a date has been tentatively assigned other than 'before 1766'. Of its two movements the second, marked *Moderato*, carries the expansion of minuet style still further (110 bars, without trio). Indeed, its soberly lyrical character enables it to combine the functions of slow movement and minuet-finale, while its calm assumption of sonata form contains other interesting points. Before the codetta material of the first half, Haydn lands on a second-position dominant seventh, elaborates it, and holds it for a minim, adding a pause-mark. This fermata, which is repeated precisely once and almost exactly once more in the second half, might perhaps be decorated in the repeats, but to embellish it the first time through would seem to destroy the original idea behind it, which is that of daringly holding up the flow of the music to create suspense – in the second half Haydn does much the same after only four bars by indulging in a completely silent bar, an effect whose purpose is only revealed when the music restarts with an expressive shift to the minor key. This *Moderato* is also significant for containing, in the surviving 70-bar fragment of autograph, a single dynamic marking (a *piano* in bar 42). Apart from being the first in the sonatas, it suggests that the dynamic markings for the first movement in the editions of the 1780s, when the work was first published, are correct. The *Allegro moderato* forming the first movement exploits many of the devices becoming familiar as Haydn develops his sonata style, with a main theme outlining the common chord of B flat major amid a welter of dotted rhythms and turns – the elaborate but still refined *galant* style lies behind much of this music, even here and there a hint of the *empfindsamkeit* (sensitivity) which was becoming such a major force in music.

Whereas in the second movement Haydn relates first and second subjects by giving them roughly similar outlines and 'scoring' them in thirds, here he uses his tripartite exposition form with great subtlety, delaying the full arrival on the dominant by means of an expressive expansion section, and linking both this and the codetta with a tag from the first theme. It is typical of his constant striving, however relaxed the music may seem, that he should combine Baroque or *galant* elements with different ways of handling the form that he himself was deriving from previous structures. His use of such standard formulae as the sequences and syncopations that are so charming in this movement pushes them towards their status as essential components in the new Classical manner he was helping to establish. He was also exploring the range of the instrument with great resourcefulness. Here is the conclusion of the *Moderato*, circling down from top F to bottom B flat:

Ex. 15   **Moderato**

In this context it is therefore a tragedy that the next seven sonatas, and most of the eighth, have been lost – their incipits, which were omitted from Päsler/Hoboken, appeared in Haydn's holograph catalogue of his works, the *Entwurf-Katalog* of c. 1765–8, and Christa Landon included them in her listing in the hope that Nos. 21–27 will some day be rediscovered in the same fortuitous way that part of No. 28 reappeared. Meanwhile one can only look at the incipits of the missing works and regret their loss – the variety indicated by the opening bars of these so-called divertimenti is considerable, including two in minor keys and one in B major, a tonic key encountered but rarely in Haydn's output (there is, for example, only one B major Symphony, No. 46). Sonata No. 28 in D appears in Hoboken's catalogue as an ensemble work in Group XIV (*Mehrstimmige Divertimenti mit Klavier*), as No. 5. Though it is listed in the *Entwurf-Katalog* as *Divertimento per il Cembalo Solo*, in the catalogue written in 1805 by his copyist Elssler and approved by Haydn himself, it can be regarded as coming under the heading of keyboard works '*Con due Violini e Basso*'. The autograph of part of the first movement's recapitulation, and the whole of a fine Menuet and trio, turned up at an auction in Marburg in 1961, and they enable us to assess the grand scale and florid nature of the approach to the first movement – the incipit, which indicates an opening theme using his favourite military dotted rhythms and arpeggiated outlines, gives no hint of the chains of scales and suspensions for which the fragment is remarkable. The noble Menuet, whose predominantly lowish register gives it an added sobriety, is allied to a superbly powerful D minor trio, the opening of which conveys the magisterial authority Haydn now commands:

Ex. 16

An extant autograph reveals the date of Sonata No. 29 in E flat (Hob. 45) as 1766 – at last, something definite! The quality of this masterly work makes the loss of the preceding sonatas even more critical in our appreciation of Haydn's development as a keyboard composer, for its three movements are unfailingly imaginative, and there is a new grandeur about the way he conveys his powers as a stylistic integrator. At the start of the first movement, *Moderato*, the repetitions of the first tiny motif build a tension released by the upward fourth in the right hand (bar 2), and the lyrical tune-like motif in bars 3–4:

Ex. 17

A repetition of this fragment characteristically extends the four-bar phrase to seven bars by sequential treatment of the unit *x* in Ex. 17. The movement contains an astonishing concentration on two-part writing, though at the start of the second subject group some Alberti bass figuration inevitably gives the texture a more chordal feeling. Here the melody line itself sounds freer, but shorn of its octave displacements and a few identical notes, is revealed simply as an oscillation between D and E flat, each melody note given half a bar, before sweeping upwards in lyrical release – it is a similar duality (stasis/motion) to that of the opening theme, to which it is also linked in other ways. A later motif in the second subject group gives a series of three descending scalic phrases followed by turns around E flat and D, reversing the process into motion/stasis. It is worth noting that the Alberti bass (not, this time, a sign of weakness) is used not only to fill out the texture but also to provide a bass line – i.e. it is both harmonic and somewhat contrapuntal (cf. bars 24–25 and elsewhere). Haydn incorporates more development of the material into the body of both exposition and recapitulation, using the modulatory transition section linking the two subject groups as an essential element in this closely-wrought movement.

The following *Andante* also concentrates on two-part writing, but again the richness and variety of the motifs, and the subtlety of the detail, prevents it from becoming too plain. In both these movements, there is a remarkable series of harmonic changes looking forward to later styles – in the *Moderato* during the recapitulation, in the *Andante* leading up to the recapitulation. Inspired touches of chromaticism, suspensions, rests in the melodic line with the effect of a singer taking a quick breath – all these give the music a rare sureness of instrumental touch and a deeply song-like feeling. The brilliant *Allegro di molto* concluding the work is a true finale as we have come to know the term, despite its quiet close. Its exuberance carries it forward through a scintillating series of ideas and developments – at several points it anticipates perhaps Haydn's greatest sonata-rondo keyboard finale, in No. 62 (also in this exceptionally successful key of E flat). It is worth noting, by the way, that the finale of No. 29 contains one of only two instances we have of Haydn's own, very practical fingering.

The first movement of Sonata No. 30 in D (Hob. 19), the autograph of which is dated 1767, is if anything even more concentrated than that of No. 29. The openings of first and second subject groups give an idea of the bold nature of the writing, as well as the fundamental melodic motifs:

Ex. 18(a)

Ex. 18(b)

(It will be noticed that Ex. 18(a), which is a complete unit of the first group, is quite firmly a three-bar phrase.) Even after the first three bars, when another idea is brought in to contrast with the opening and make up the initial body of the first group, repeated bass notes anticipate the most striking feature of the second subject group, the repeated notes of Ex. 18(b). What is being termed here a 'second subject group' is, at the same time, the start of a massive expansion section arriving at a firm root-position dominant only after 14½ bars for the lengthy closing section. In various transformations, the melodic outlines of Ex. 18(a), either in prime form (right hand) or inverted (as in the left hand, with slight deviations), govern a great deal of the thematic working of the movement, while the textures of Ex. 18(b) give it much of its driving force and strength of character. In the development section, bar 53 onwards, there is a sustained growth of expressive intensification posi-

33

tively demanding the gradual *crescendo* available on the piano rather than the sharply segregated dynamics of the earlier keyboard instruments. In the slow movement, however, the extreme changes of register may indicate the specific influence of (especially) the clavichord, on which the contrasts emerge with vital clarity – the modern pianist must be aware of this, and try to achieve something of the same effect by intensifying the touch and tone-colouring of the performance.

Despite its undoubted qualities, notably the demonstration of Haydn's growing ability to make an expansive movement out of short and often germinal ideas, I find myself unable to warm to the *Moderato*, and the same is true of the succeeding *Andante*. Here the influence of C. P. E. Bach can surely be felt in the extraordinary leaps in the bass and some striking and lengthy passages with both hands in the bass clef – the main theme, too, starting with repeated notes reminds one of the *Moderato*, helping to bind the work together. Yet it seems overlong for its material, and too consistently dark and heavy in texture. The real delight of the sonata is the *Allegro assai* finale – this marks the introduction into the sonatas of a favourite form, a cross between rondo and variations with each ritornello section genuinely a variation of the main theme and each episode contrasting in some way. There are three episodes: a pleasantly dramatic one in D minor, largely in octaves introducing a tone of mock-drama into the proceedings, a vigorous and pounding one in A in which the melodic outlines recall Ex. 18(a), and (not really a separate episode at all) a skeletal repetition in octaves of the first half of the main tune in the middle of its final variation. It makes a brilliant, highly entertaining finish to a work to which, despite the thematic cross-references, it doesn't seem quite to belong.

The Middle Period: (i) Sonatas L. 31–33

If the influence of C. P. E. Bach has already been felt in such pieces as the slow movement of Sonata No. 30, or the elaborately decorative nature of the welter of turns around the dotted rhythms at the start of No. 20, it is more evident in the next three works, which, though not specifically connected, it seems sensible to group together here. They form an astonishing and exciting leap forward in style and technique. It is a pity that no autograph exists for No. 31 in A flat (Hob. 46), but it was designated in the *Entwurf-Katalog* as about 1767/68, and this dating seems generally agreed. One is surprised at such a relatively early date for it, since its majestic proportions and maturity of expression might suggest that it was composed later – it is a masterpiece of a very high order, the first Haydn sonata to which one can unequivocally assign such praise. His preoccupations in the period starting in the late 1760s are clearly shown in other genres, the *Sturm und Drang* symphonies, for instance, and the quartets, especially those of Opp. 17 and 20 – they include a new interest in contrapuntal formulae, notably in the fugues of the Op. 20 quartets, and the heightened emotional content which music was now being used to express. But he continued to integrate elements from previous traditions and techniques along with the new, and this stylistic synthesis was never achieved more impressively than in these three works.

The A flat Sonata opens with a vast *Allegro moderato*, placing before us a wide variety of motifs and containing a development section lasting 39 bars – the sheer size of the movement might persuade pianists not to make the second repeat, but I believe that it is preferable to perform it in full if possible, for this emphasises the magisterial progress of the music. It is in sonata form and exploits to the full the contemporary keyboard range, with some striking concentrations of texture with both hands in either treble or bass clef. The opening theme (Ex. 19 below) consists of a three-bar phrase beginning on the tonic and ending with a tonic cadence, followed by a five-bar phrase again ending on the tonic. There is a mildness, an apparent lack of energy, in these cadences which, though the melodic lines themselves have a fine lyrical sweep, might lead one to expect a decorative, amiable movement, possibly quite modestly proportioned. The sextuplets beginning the second (five-bar) phrase soon take over and start to propel the music forwards, leading to a strong cadence over a B flat pedal and a pause. The second subject has now been reached, in the dominant, but on reflection the first 17 bars are not simply a collection of decorative phrases and scales (though often performed as if they are merely an excuse for the pianist to demonstrate a pearly touch) but rather a slowly evolving but ultimately powerful growth towards something more substantial. The phrases ending on simple tonic cadences are *not* separate, they are blocks in the construction of an edifice. Even the very first phrase itself contains a sense of forward motion with its increase of pace in the main melody notes from half a bar each to a quarter of a bar each and, finally, to the final dotted rhythm:

Ex. 19

When we reach the second subject itself, there is a change of register from the strong bass-clef cadence preceding it to a lighter, airier texture in the treble. Here the sextuplets serve to provide forward momentum for a theme that seems at first static and only moves away after a couple of bars:

Ex. 20

The left hand contributes as much to the theme as the right, and when the sextuplets take over and move the music forward it is only for it to sweep down and then up again to reach another pause, this time on a sustained chord and thus an opportunity for some embellishment, certainly in the repeat. These pauses occur in the same positions in the recapitulation, and in the development there are three more: one in a position analogous to the rest before the second subject, and two on chords forming crucial points in the exceptionally free, fantasia-like passage when the music is moving towards the recapitulation. Haydn's special way of using pauses and rests (silence, in other words) to provide moments of dramatic or, in other contexts, humorous tension (where the music is, as it were, still going on *through* the pause) is developing.

The exploratory, gradually-unfolding nature of the *Allegro*, and the fantasia-like episodes, undoubtedly owe a debt to C. P. E. Bach, whom Haydn greatly admired. They allow him an exceptional degree of freedom in his handling of the form, and also permit the development section a remarkable and impressive series of chord changes, using a Baroque toccata figuration to carry the music inexorably forward. Here is the harmonic outline of this rich passage:

Ex. 21

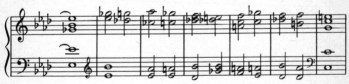

This is the most powerful example of the movement's intensity, but many other details, chromatic inflections or changes of rhythm, enrich it – in the recapitulation, the main theme's reappearance first in the tonic major and then, memorably, in A flat minor is one such touching moment. It is an intimate and at the same time a massive piece.

The following *Adagio* has the same qualities, a heart-rendingly beautiful intimacy of tone and yet an expansive, richly-worked tapestry of ideas. The opening is unique in his sonatas for its layout:

Ex. 22

This passacaglia-like left-hand line is then repeated, with the loveliest of counter-melodies above it. After this, the movement assumes its predominant three-part texture, including a glorious sequence of trills, suspensions and scales clearly related to Ex. 20 but occupying quite a different world – the melodic line itself is woven in and out of the accompanying decoration in the subtlest, most magical way, demanding acute perception of balance from the player. The contrapuntal richness of the development is deeply moving, and so is the imaginative sequential handling of Ex. 22 leading back to the suspensions and trills:

Ex. 23

There is an even more evocative and inspired series of harmonic changes (and enharmonic shifts) before the fermata preceding the final cadence. This *Adagio* remains one of the loveliest of all Haydn's slow movements.

In the final *Presto*, we have a characteristically boisterous sonata-rondo, both repeats of which need to be observed if it is to fulfil its proper place in the overall scheme of the work. It is one of the best of its kind, using Baroque sequences and figurations with freshness, and once again scales provide a genuine motive force. Its high spirits give it an irresistible charm, and it makes a perfect conclusion to the sonata – its brilliance has sufficient power to match the greater emotional weight of the other movements.

The intimacy noted in the A flat Sonata is even more marked in the G minor Sonata that follows it in Christa Landon's edition, No. 32 (Hob. 44). It is worth mentioning here that its provisional dating of 1768–70 is questioned by some authorities, notably Charles Rosen, in his fine book, *The Classical Style* (Faber and Faber, 1971). The work's intensely personal feeling is enhanced by the lack of an exuberant finale – there are only two movements, a *Moderato* imbued with the subtlest and most delicate pathos, and an *Allegretto* which, though slightly more forthright, sustains the mood of emotional intensity. The *Allegretto*, indeed, is really a minuet in G minor returning, after a trio clearly based on a related theme, in an elaborate variation, followed by a brief, varied of part of the trio again to form a kind of coda to the sonata. This extends the capabilities of the minuet style, not merely in decorating and varying the material, but also in enabling such a movement to bear a greater share of the emotional significance of the work as a whole.

Nevertheless it is in the first movement that the importance of this lovely work largely rests, and it is surprising, in view of its poised beauty, that so few pianists have taken it up (despite the example given by Sviatoslav Richter's classic recording). The seriousness and depth displayed here match, if indeed they do not excel, that of Haydn's other fine G minor works of the period, such as the *Stabat Mater* and the Symphony No. 39, and it is once again extremely resourceful in its use of keyboard timbres. Haydn uses very simple materials to build a structure of considerable complexity – simple step-wise movement for the main part of the opening theme, for example, or downward arpeggio flourishes for the second subject. The tone is of a deep, rather veiled sadness, which does not preclude him from building up at the end of the development a massive climactic phrase of real power that fits in magically with the context of the movement: it is as if the grandeur of this moment is just below the surface all the time, and it is based on the triplet up-beat to the main theme:

Ex. 24

The recapitulation starts at once with the opening phrase heard an octave lower, giving it an added richness and emotional force. It is to be noted also that before the coda Haydn writes out a right-hand cadenza above a sustained diminished chord, marking it *sempre più adagio*, the first time he has employed this Baroque tradition in this way in the sonatas.

The C minor Sonata, No. 33 (Hob. 20), is the first to have established itself in the repertoire. It represents Haydn's deepest keyboard excursion into the world of *Sturm und Drang* (Storm and Stress), the artistic movement that was to last longer in literature than in music and to which Goethe was a major contributor. To over-simplify grossly, it replaced the 'objectivity' of the Baroque and pre-Classical styles with a new 'subjectivity', a new expression of personal feelings in place of what its propagators saw as the blandness of previous styles. The Age of Enlightenment was to be replaced by a literary age in which impulse, feeling and instinct were seen as links between man and divine nature. In music, C. P. E. Bach, whose profound influence on Haydn has already been noted, led the way with his elaborate, often disturbingly irrational, deeply expressive works – indeed, the whole movement had its fullest musical expression before it had really begun to flourish in literature. In Haydn's output it is the symphonies and quartets from the late 1760s and early 1770s that show it most frequently – such works as Symphonies Nos. 44 in E minor (the *Trauer-Sinfonie* or Mourning Symphony) or 49 in F minor (*La Passione*) and the minor-key quartets.

He combined this heightened emotional content with, interestingly enough, an almost self-conscious interest in Baroque contrapuntal forms, just as did some of his contemporaries (d'Ordoñez and Gassmann, for example). It was the fusion of the newly-discovered emotional capabilities of music with elements from Rococo and Baroque technique that finally created the Viennese Classical style as inherited by Mozart and Beethoven in their maturity.

In this context the C minor Sonata achieves a unique position in the sonatas, for it is Haydn's only such work from the height of this period. There are later works breathing the same intensely emotional air, such as the B minor (No. 47) and the C sharp minor (No. 49) sonatas, but their forms are more classically balanced. It is interesting to compare the finales of the C minor and C sharp minor sonatas. Both derive a strong impetus from the rhythmic motif ♩ ♩ ♪ accompanying their opening themes – in the later work it is part of a classically shaped, quite traditional Menuet and trio of considerable emotional force. In the C minor, the underlying minuet-style is transformed into something far more complex, both structurally and expressively. Coincidentally, both sonatas were published in the same set by Artaria in 1780 (No. 33 along with Nos. 48–52). The C minor is the first to be entitled Sonata, instead of the terms partita or divertimento used before, and it is also the first to contain detailed dynamic markings. These give rise to some speculation about the instrument for which it was intended. Artaria marked the set 'Per il Clavicembalo, o Forte Piano', obviously aiming at as wide a circulation as possible – in his edition, *crescendi* and other markings certainly suggest the use of a Hammerklavier. But the surviving fragment of autograph bears the heading for 'Clavi Cembalo', which might suggest harpsichord – Christa Landon, in the introduction to her edition, inclines to the view that, since the dynamic marks often contradict the indication for a harpsichord, we should regard 'Clavi Cembalo' as being simply 'a genre description for keyboard instruments'.

The extraordinary richness of this sonata lies in its multitude of thematic motifs, an immense variety of moods and textures handled in a brief time-span, and great formal resourcefulness, in which Haydn's treatment of harmonic movement is not the least remarkable feature. Along with this widening of expressive musical horizons, he achieves a synthesis of past elements – the concertante style of C. P. E. Bach's concerti distinctly colours the work, notably at the two cadential points in the first movement when, shortly before the codetta and again prior to the coda, the music comes to rest on a dominant-ninth chord, marked *adagio* and lightly decorated. Rococo decoration still plays an important part in his material, and in the slow movement there is a strong Baroque strain. From the very opening (*Moderato* in the autograph, *Allegro moderato* in the first edition) we are plunged straight into a world of the most exquisite emotional sensibility, even drama – there is an almost bewildering array of motifs and textures in the first 20 bars. The movement is in sonata form, of course, but what a web of motifs go to make it!

Ex. 25(a)

Ex. 25(b)

Ex. 25(c)

The placing of the second subject alone shows Haydn's inventiveness. It begins in bar 15 (Ex. 25(c) above) on a dominant seventh chord of B flat, resolving into the 'correct' tonality of E flat (second inversion) only in the next bar, a device helping to disguise the start of the theme – but by this time the listener has been so unsettled anyway that one is hardly aware of any new material starting until it is well under way. (In this case, I am firmly persuaded that this is a genuine second subject rather than an expansion section.)

The first subject group has two distinct parts. The first is made up of a four-bar phrase followed by another of four bars sub-divided into two which are more contrasted with each other and cover a rise and fall of well over an octave in the right hand and over two octaves in the left. In bar 9 the second phase of the first group begins (Ex. 25(b)), this time two three-bar phrases. The right-hand melisma in the second and third bars of these phrases leads quite naturally into the second subject (Ex. 25(c)), the end of which is as open as the beginning, since it leads to a lengthy build-up and examination of the dominant-ninth chord, with cadenza, mentioned above. Perhaps the most fascinating feature of this exposition section is the way Haydn, having by great diversity of rhythm and texture driven the music to this cadential point, comes to rest on a dominant pedal for, in effect, 13 bars (more than one-third of the total length of the exposition). There are departures from it: in the decoration before the *adagio* cadenza the bass wavers between B flat and C flat before coming to rest on the former, and after the prolonged pause on the dominant ninth Haydn moves off *tempo primo* (and *forte*) with a conventional cadence figure leading to a dominant seventh on B flat, this time as a device to move to the sunnier climes of E flat for the codetta. Haydn has thus used the pedal note expressively (the hovering to and from C flat is marvellously touching) and later changed it into a vacillation between the bass of the E flat second inversion and the bass of a dominant seventh to delay as long as possible the resolution. It is a daring, courageous passage and one maintaining the tension created from the start of the sonata by the sheer intensity.

The mixture of elements making up the material is tremendous – the Exx. 25 show some of them. But there are also many inter-relationships in the ideas. The four-note tag x in Ex. 25(a), for instance, clearly emerges in 25(b) and 25(c), especially with the added repetition of its last note to make this clearer, and it forms the main motif in the codetta, this time at quadruple its original speed and placed above an Alberti-style bass. The use of thirds and sixths, which appear extensively in both first and second subjects, is another unifying force, and even the tiny little tag with which the exposition ends employs thirds anticipating what comes next, whether in the first section repeat or the start of the development. Furthermore, the dotted rhythm, so stately in bar 1, is employed at double or even quadruple speed intermittently, as well as reappearing naturally in the restatements of the main theme. The flow of the music is so emotionally rich and full of musical incident that it sounds as free as a fantasia, yet it is actually as concentrated and controlled a piece as any in Haydn's output. The development section is, technically, more straightforward – after three brief, increasingly tense references to the main theme in E flat, F minor and A flat, the music settles on B flat minor for a development of the codetta figure based on x above an Alberti bass. This is then repeated in E flat minor, but now extended and turning into a marvellous flowering of the lyrical line above constant left-hand sextuplets, first through a series of wonderful harmonic changes and then through a period when it seems to be settling into E flat, to a superbly shaped and elongated cadence into G minor.

It is at this point that Haydn produces perhaps his most inspired structural twist, for having reached the dominant key and the point at which the recapitulation is due, he radically alters the conventional format. There is, indeed, some disagreement about precisely where the recapitulation *does* start – Charles Rosen, in the sleevenotes to his CBS recording, states: 'When the main theme returns . . . it is dramatically but sparsely rewritten, *starting with its second phase.*' [My italics.] This is bars 65–68, two two-bar phrases derived from Ex. 25(b) and moving first to D minor and then to the tonic, C minor. Haydn also changes the order of events within these phrases – the equivalent of bar 9, formerly the start of this phrase, forms the second bar (i.e. the end, since it has been telescoped from three bars to two) and is preceded by one melismatic bar derived from bar 10. Technically speaking, I suppose this is indeed the recapitulation, with Haydn changing the order in which the various phases of the first subject group appear, but it always seems to me that only with the reappearance of the first phase (Ex. 25(a)) in the tonic key does one really *hear* the recapitulation as beginning. Whatever the correct answer, the fact remains that Haydn is characteristically dovetailing the sections, and though the recapitulation is condensed it still contains moments of yet more development which add to the profound impression that this wonderful movement makes. Even the little codetta tag is developed a bit at the close, as if reluctant to bring this deeply emotional piece to an end.

The first movement, full of passionate intensity even when at its most restrained, and the finale, so powerfully and defiantly tragic, are contrasted types of *Sturm und Drang*, but the slow movement openly avows the influence of the High Baroque in the evenly flowing lines which pursue their serene path through this *Andante con moto*, in the considerable use of the written-out rubato provided by syncopations, and in the apparently inexhaustible subtlety of the sequential development. Charles Rosen aptly describes it as 'a still centre for the storm of the two outer movements', and it is by its sheer contrast, the necessity for such a point of repose, and the heavenly beauty of its melodic lines in both hands, that it fits so miraculously into the sonata. Haydn surrounds the flowing accompaniment, often enriched by the parallel thirds which are such an important textural element in the first movement, with a melodic line that is both embroidered and expressive. The sonata form adopted once again dovetails development and recapitulation in a seamless flow which at one point takes the right hand soaring upwards with scales wreathed in trills while the left hand descends in thirds to a beat where the two hands are four octaves apart, an adventurous and striking texture.

The final *Allegro* plunges us back into turbulence – it is an unrelenting outburst of impassioned rhetoric, expressed in terms of the utmost formal cohesion and great technical virtuosity. The sonata-rondo form enables Haydn once more to compress the two recapitulatory sections while still varying their material, and the two main thematic forces behind the movement are (i) the opening theme, with descending scale figures usually of five notes and clearly akin to the tag *x* in Ex. 25(a), and (ii) a virtuosic display of ascending semiquavers. There are more lyrical moments, but it is these two ideas which provide the main motive force, and a good deal of the sense of struggle conveyed by the music derives from the contrast between the downward motion of one and the upward striving of the other. Once again thirds are an important part of the texture – they accompany the main theme and, apart from other appearances, provide the flowing codetta/coda material. Since this is a sonata-rondo, there can be two 'development' sections. The first of these includes some marvellously forward-looking two-part writing (another typical example of Haydn's use of a Baroque technique to serve his new expressive needs), and the second builds up to a massive climax in which toccata figuration, involving much crossing of hands, explores a rich series of harmonies looking back to Bach and yet forward to Schumann. The technical difficulty of this section matches the heightened passion of the music. Here is the harmonic scheme – it is worth emphasising that the chords last one bar each save for the penultimate one which, lasting two bars, screws up the tension almost unbearably before the resolution of the cadence:

Ex. 26

Up to this point in his keyboard music Haydn had never before demanded quite so much from his performers – it was to be a long time before he demanded so much again.

The Middle Period: (ii) L. 34–41

The Sonatas in D major and A flat major, Nos. 34 and 35 (Hob. 33 and 43), first appeared in print in London in 1783, along with the E minor (No. 53), but there seems little doubt that they date from the early 1770s. Both are relatively light, insignificant works, compared to the three just discussed. Indeed, the change of tone is startling – it is almost as if the experiences which left their mark on those works had never occurred (Haydn's illness in 1770 certainly had influenced the C minor). Were it not that many of the next twenty or so sonatas are as light as these two, one would doubt such a late dating – but the surprising feature of Haydn's sonata output is that, after reaching such a pinnacle of achievement, he did not develop further and produce a series of masterpieces, as he did in the symphonies and quartets, but was content to explore his techniques more modestly in the keyboard works. That most of them were written for amateurs (many of them aristocratic young ladies) would explain this to some extent, and it is a pity that this sudden change of approach to the sonata has led to an under-estimation of the very real qualities of many of them. Despite their modesty, several of them reward the closest attention – it is noteworthy that Sviatoslav Richter, whose choice of Haydn sonatas had been more extensive and imaginative than that of any other major pianist, has performed (and in some cases recorded) a substantial number of this middle group of works.

The opening *Allegro* of No. 34 really deserves *giocoso* as a tempo marking – starting with a rhythmic figure ♫♫ (with which Nos. 4 and 18 also began and which played an important part in several early works), it is a witty and diverting movement, using pauses and hesitations to point up the discreet humour characterising it. The move to B minor at the start of the development is strikingly achieved, above an F sharp pedal which offers a dramatic surprise in this context. The *Adagio* is a different matter. In D minor, it has a powerful main theme with an extraordinary resemblance to the B flat major episode in Mozart's C minor Fantasia (K. 475), written in 1785, and is both spacious and deeply expressive – it has great clarity of texture, richness of harmony and a wide keyboard range (in one place, the hands are four-and-a-half octaves apart). It leads without a break into the finale, a *Tempo di Menuet* consisting of a typical form of alternating variations (purely decorative in this instance) on two themes, the first in D major, the second D minor.

The A flat major Sonata No. 35 starts with a *Moderato* theme oddly similar to the first of the variation tunes from No. 34's finale, at any rate for a few bars. This work is more consistent in inspiration than its predecessor – the opening movement is full of sturdy purposefulness and handles sonata form with Haydn's customary imagination (the second subject group is virtually a reworking of the first, and plays little part in the recapitulation). The second movement is a *Menuetto* with a strong rhythmic impulse akin to the scherzo style of Beethoven's Bagatelle, Op. 33 No. 2, while the trio is decidedly *ländlerisch*. The entertaining finale is a *Presto* given, for the first time, the title Rondo, though there is only one distinct episode, a rumbustious outburst in F minor. A later episode sounds more like a coda but turns into a development of earlier material to take us back to yet another delightful variation of the main theme, made even wittier by some amusing octave displacements, and a supremely witty finish.

The first authentic printing of Haydn sonatas, and the first edition supervised by him, came from the Viennese publisher Kurzböck in 1774, the set of six sonatas written the previous year, Nos. 36–41 (Hob. 21–26). Curiously enough, Mozart's set of six sonatas, K. 279–284, showing clearly Haydn's influence, date from 1774/75. The dedication of Haydn's set is to Prince Nicolaus Esterházy, who would certainly have enjoyed the delicacy and wide range of forms they display, as well as their considerable intellectual content. No. 36 in C (Hob. 21) is lively and springy, deriving much of its first movement character from the divertimento style, with dotted rhythms and decorative, *galant* ornamentation written into the melodic outlines of the triplets which enter the texture with the second subject group. The beginning of this, however, is merely the same as the first bar of the first subject, in the dominant, and the triplets really take charge for the elegant and witty codetta, here unusually extended. The succeeding *Adagio* is resonant, with full chords at crucial moments (Haydn's placing of a strong diminished seventh chord to create momentary suspense and deepen the music's impact is especially fine). There are occasional pre-echoes of Beethoven – indeed, it might not be presumptuous to suggest that in its ornamentation the *Adagio* looks as much forward to the later master as back to the Rococo. The *Presto* finale reverts to the familiar 3/8 style and is characterised particularly by mordents, both written-out and merely indicated – it is a brilliant, light-hearted movement in which the second subject is simply a stronger, canonic reworking of the first, this time in thirds. One delightful touch is a cunning modulation to A minor in the development – it is only the relative minor, after all, and thus an obvious key to approach, but the context is cleverly arranged to make it sound momentarily rather exotic and unexpected.

The E major Sonata No. 37 (Hob. 22) is richer, however, with greater emotional warmth. This is especially true of the outer movements. The opening *Allegro moderato* starts with a sunny and elaborate theme using written-out turns as an essential part of its line – such is its sense of completeness, aided by a full chord at the start of each phrase, that Haydn can rely on a simple, but expressive, rising sequence for the start of the second subject group (an expansion section in harmonic technique, starting with a first-inversion dominant), in the course of which, prior to the codetta, he demonstrates his delight at exploiting witty and interesting keyboard textures:

Ex. 27

Instead of starting the development in the dominant key of B, reached at the end of the exposition, Haydn achieves a powerful effect by plunging into G sharp minor (first inversion), which, it becomes apparent, is a dramatic device having two effects: that of moving to the tonic's relative minor (C sharp) and that of widening the music's emotional horizons. The finale is marked *Tempo di Menuet*, and it inherits from that form both the elegant character of the E major main theme and the somewhat trio-like feeling of the more dramatic E minor section which follows. In reality, this is an alternating rondo-variation structure, three versions of the main theme separated by E minor couplets with their own material in common, ending with the third version of the major key section and a witty final cadence. The *Andante* forming the centre-piece of this lovely work is a flowing E minor arioso almost continuously derived from melodic triplets. There is much sequential or contrapuntal development of this, and a beautifully-placed dotted rhythm which appears only four times in the whole movement but lights up and expands its subtle impact in a way that performers can help to clarify by emphasising this rhythmic differentiation.

The typical Austrian dotted march rhythms start Sonata No. 38 in F (Hob. 23), one of the more frequently performed of these works, with a tune vividly recalling the very first sonata of all, but as with No. 36 the rhythmic emphasis gradually changes, in this instance from dotted rhythms through level semiquavers to rippling demisemiquavers which become predominant. It is a lively, exuberant piece, several times taking sudden but entirely convincing plunges into more dramatic atmospheres – there is an effective sideways step into A flat in the recapitulation, and, at a roughly analogous spot in the recapitulation, a right-hand cadenza above a sustained left-hand trill. After this quite powerful and virtuosic piece, the following siciliano-like *Adagio* has a touchingly sweet sadness – here too, this time over a sustained octave pedal note, there is a free-sounding right-hand melisma before the close. This movement clearly influenced Mozart, as did the genuinely symphonic finale, perhaps the first in a Haydn sonata to relate so directly to his mature orchestral finale manner. It is delightfully bold – not least for beginning the development section on a diminished seventh chord, kept going for no less than six bars before resolving. The work's popularity is hardly surprising.

The variety of this set of sonatas is shown by the utterly different nature of the D major, No. 39 (Hob. 24). Here, Haydn balances the work by giving us a spacious, wonderfully lyrical *Allegro* followed by two shorter movements, a fragile and warmly expressive *Adagio* leading to a delightful *Presto* finale. I must confess to a particular fondness, even among so many fine pieces, for this sonata – it is imbued with a unique, luminous grace. This is not to say that it lacks drama or virtuosity, for the *Allegro* uses toccata figuration to build and create powerful tension, but it never goes beyond the bounds of what is apt in a predominantly lyrical work. The exposition is a fascinating example of Haydn's subtle integration of closely-related structures. It starts with the first subject group: two four-bar phrases, repeated, followed by a repeated two-bar answering phrase finished with a half-close. Immediately, in the (unprepared) dominant, the second part of the exposition starts, with a transposition of the opening theme changing to a cadential figure, and then the toccata figuration just mentioned. The final section of the exposition begins (still in the dominant) with a variant of the equable quavers from the first theme and then moves back into the toccata style. Even the two final phrases, both cadential in manner, refer back to these two important elements.

Haydn starts the development with some canons set perfectly into their context – note that on the first main beat, the right hand turns the conventional dominant into a seventh, pushing the tonality back to the tonic:

Ex. 28

The three movements have in common an interrupted cadence at an important point, but these serve different expressive purposes (in the finale it is part of a monumental and irresistible joke). The *Adagio*'s opening theme, in D minor, is extraordinarily delicate, with its halting, pathetic tune above a simple, Baroque accompaniment – its restatement in F, as a more continuous line with flowing accompaniment, is like a ray of sunshine, even more beautifully judged than a similar change of key at a similar place in No. 38's slow movement. The finale is equally and inspiredly simple, two variants of a binary first section which I cannot forebear from quoting, to give a taste of the sensitivity and grace of the music:

Ex. 29

Neither of the two remaining sonatas of this set maintains the balance or sustained inspiration of the others, though naturally they contain much of interest. The first movement, *Moderato*, of the E flat Sonata No. 40 (Hob. 25) is indeed full of remarkable features. It opens with a strong theme of remarkably 'public' nature, against the more intimate nature of the sonatas hitherto – the anticipation of some of Beethoven's gestures is reinforced not only by the dotted rhythms heard almost immediately afterwards (vividly recalling the *Vivace alla Marcia* of the A major Sonata, Op. 101), but also by the resounding restatement of the opening bars in bass octaves beneath florid decoration, looking forward also to the grandeur of Haydn's last E flat sonata. The problem for the performer is tempo, for a speed that seems right for the opening is not necessarily suitable for the elaborate passagework to come – this can easily become hectic rather than vigorous. The writing is certainly grand, with an unexpected reliance on octave doublings even in the thematic outline of much of the passagework, and if perhaps it contains too much diverse material which Haydn seems unable to unify with his customary skill, it surely marks a step forward in his growth to a bigger keyboard style. The only other movement is marked *Tempo di Menuet*, and is a straightforward minuet without trio, written in his mature and forthright manner with one important new feature: it is almost entirely canonic, the right hand leading the first part and the left hand leading the second. This conscious incorporation into the sonata of more or less strict canon was to become an important feature of Clementi's work – the enormous *Allegro* third movement of his G major sonata, Op. 40 no. 1, is in effect a Menuet and trio exploiting this to the utmost. Haydn himself, as early as the late 1750s, had used canonic imitation as a technique in the Menuet of his String Quartet, Op. 1 No. 1, and it is odd that it was so long before he applied it to his keyboard writing.

The A major Sonata, No. 41 (Hob. 26), also contains, as the middle movement, a Menuet and trio, both labelled *al Rovescio* and derived from the same movement in the Symphony No. 47 in G – they are palindromic (i.e. the second half is the first backwards), and have inspired Robert Simpson to write two sets of variations on the minuet, the early work for piano and the magnificent String Quartet No. 9 (1982), a work of monumental size. The first movement of the sonata is substantial and charming, with a faintly military air to its determined first subject and a wealth of material far more unified than in the previous work's *Moderato* – only what seems to me an over-reliance on fairly straightforward sequences in the development weakens it. The balance of the work, too, is less than convincing, for the quirky minuet and the single page of *Presto* finale do not manage to balance either structurally or stylistically the large-scale, finely worked *Allegro moderato* – though it should be added that the finale's brevity and naïvety (the main theme is virtually a scale down and then a scale up) makes it extremely amusing in its own right. As a whole, the work is strongly coloured by implications of the sharply-etched, clearly-differentiated harpsichord or clavichord sound, in contrast to the more pianistic manner displayed in the next group of sonatas.

The Middle Period: (iii) L. 42–47

These were published by Haydn himself in manuscript copies in 1776, though it is known that some of them date from earlier, perhaps even from 1770. They have no dedication. There was a mischievous attempt by the *European Magazine and London Review* in 1784 to create the myth that these and the previous set were written as deliberate parodies of C. P. E. Bach, which would thus account for the 'capricious manner, odd breaks, whimsical modulations, and very often childish manner, mixed with an affectation of profound science'. This article was widely disseminated in both England and Germany, obliging C. P. E. Bach to declare publicly his admiration for Haydn and to disown the imputation of having written unfavourably about him. The magnificent quality of these sonatas in any case gives the lie to the article. They share something of the relaxed tone of their predecessors, but on the whole their scope is grander, the keyboard writing still more adventurous, the invention as fertile and varied as ever. It might even be argued that the sonatas of this period, though not so massive as the C minor or some of the last works, sustain a higher level of inspiration than (with notable exceptions) the symphonies of the same decade. It is worth noting that only one, the E major, lacks a minuet of some kind (Haydn's development of this form achieves a marvellous richness in this set), yet only one, the F major, has a genuine slow movement – such is the depth of imagination in these works that the lack of this is hardly noticed.

The set opens with a bracing G major work, No. 42 (Hob. 27) – the nautical adjective occurs because the simple phrase with which the second subject group commences is to be found later in that splendid Victorian ballad *The Death of Nelson*. The *Allegro con brio* starts vigorously with a jolly tune employing scales, decorated with turns, and repeated notes – in the second subject group the Alberti bass accompaniment appears, and this, beneath broken chords, drives the development along energetically. There are a few hints of chromaticism, a few implications of minor keys, but generally the music is fresh and open. So is the graceful Menuet, and though the trio starts in G minor, its second part opens with a warm B flat major motif above an amiably bassoon-like pedal texture. The final *Presto* is a highly entertaining romp through a series of variations on a rondo-style tune that closely resembles the one in the finale of Sonata No. 38 in F. This is a thoroughly characteristic Haydn finale form, aptly described by William S.

Newman: 'a special kind of variation form that sounds almost as much like a rondo. In this form his theme is the sort of tune that would be ideal for a rondo refrain except that it divides into two equal or unequal, repeated "halves". Since the B part of this theme makes a clear and tonal contrast to the A part, each variation on the A–B theme starts by giving the impression of a return to a refrain (A). The variations are of a relatively brilliant sort, suitable in a finale, and full of syncopations, figural elaborations, and articulatory refinements.' One interesting point about this exciting finale is that Haydn changes dramatically to the minor key a quarter of the way through the third of the four variations, something he does rarely but which is effective in giving the music an extra impulse – normally, such changes occur at the beginning of variations.

Exactly the same form, with the same delightful shift to the minor key, inhabits the *Presto* finale to the next sonata, No. 43 (Hob. 28), one of the fine series of E flat works. As always with his sonatas in this key there is an extra grandeur, perhaps even a touch of severity, about it, though any austerity is softened by charming inflections of warmth or humour. The central Menuet, for instance, has a certain brusqueness, turned into something more affecting by the move to the minor mode for the middle part, and the E flat minor trio is deeply expressive as well as highly imaginative in its implied shifts of metre from triple to duple time with some overlapping phrases. The opening *Allegro moderato* is extraordinarily rich in material. The first subject starts with a powerful striding theme incorporating broken chords first in the left hand and then the right – it also contains within its first phase an important sequential figure based on repeated notes (mostly in sixths) and suspensions, with a 'Scotch snap' rhythm. The second phase repeats the first two bars but then goes into a motif based on trills and scales. There is a third phase (turning into a transition section), starting in C minor, before the music moves to B flat major for the second subject, a sprightly theme in thirds. The codetta is largely derived from the trills and 'Scotch snap' from the first subject group, and the development shows Haydn's skill at keeping the music flowing with seeming spontaneity while employing an almost bewildering diversity of motifs. But perhaps the most striking feature of the work is the actual theme of the finale, almost a two-part invention or dialogue between the two hands, with part A consisting of two six-bar phrases and part B one ten-bar phrase. Out of such apparently simple material Haydn fashions variations of vivacity and complexity:

Ex. 30

Even more than with the previous set, one could indicate the variety of these works simply by giving their incipits, but for the F major Sonata, No. 44 (Hob. 29), this would hardly convey the true greatness of this extraordinary piece. For its first movement alone it would occupy a high place in Haydn's output, but the *Adagio* and finale maintain this level. The first movement is marked *Moderato*, and in its juxtaposition of totally different textures and rhythms, its dramatic modulations, and its apparent eccentricity it reveals once again the influence of both C. P. E. Bach and the Mannheimers – indeed, in some respects it belongs among the *Sturm und Drang* works. It starts with a theme[1] comprising several important motifs: a dotted rhythm followed by a lyrical phrase using appoggiaturas in the right hand, above a doggedly repeated F in the bass, the first phrase being rounded off by the dotted rhythm in deep bass thirds. A figure elegantly curling round and then step-wise downwards is also important in the first subject group. After a pause, the second group starts with a flourish of arpeggios, all in the treble, and a little downwards scale using the 'Scotch snap' rhythm. This part leads to an amazing little bridge-passage based on a single repeated note which gradually increases pace (and in the development to lead to the recapitulation is surrounded by others also spreading wider to enable a modulation to return to the tonic); the codetta is mainly lyrical and somewhat ornate. It is a quirky and entertaining exposition, full of variety and the contrast between the three main groups of

1   A more elegiac version of which opens the superb F sharp major Piano Trio written in London in 1794/5.

material, which hardly prepares us for the explosive version of the start
commencing the development. Starting in C minor, it immediately
switches to A flat and then to a diminished seventh chord to lead to the
appoggiaturas in a dark and sombre G minor. No sooner have we begun
to feel that the development has now settled down than another dramatic seventh chord leads to D minor, and only now does this section start
moving forwards. A mere verbal description cannot give an adequate
idea of the power of this section, nor can it convey fully the satisfaction
achieved by the cunningly organised return to the opening for the
recapitulation (which typically develops some of the material still
more), nor indeed the sense with which the movement gradually falls
into place after this as a real, coherent entity instead of merely a
collection of often disparate ideas.

The *crescendo* marking in bar 22 is authentic, suggesting that Haydn
had the fortepiano in mind when writing the piece. So does the sonorous
nature of the wonderful slow movement which, for all its Baroque
decorative elements, is a great classical *Adagio*, perfectly proportioned
and both grave and sensitive in expression. Here again the handling of
tonality is subtle and dramatic – the brief 'development' section (simply
a five-bar interlude) begins on a dominant seventh with a reference to
the lovely second subject and ends, via a typical Neapolitan cadence,
quite firmly in D major. After a rest, the recapitulation starts equally
firmly in B flat major, the *Adagio*'s home key – a bold and profound
juxtaposition, as dramatic in its way as the sudden move from B flat to D
in the first movement of the *Hammerklavier* Sonata (bar 37). In the finale,
Haydn gives us a *Tempo di Menuet* which in itself is elaborate and striking
– there are two increasingly ornate variations on it, and a final variation
of the second of its two parts to extend the phraseology of the movement
and emphasise its finality. It makes an excellent finish, for its descent
from straightforward minuet tradition is combined with a truly large-
scale investigation of the material, and particularly fine is the F minor
trio section, which only occurs once (after the Minuet in its original
form). Here Haydn indulges once more in some metrical dislocation
underlining the deeply expressive nature of the music:

Ex. 31

The next two sonatas do not attempt the same complex scale — indeed, the A major, No. 45 (Hob. 30), is almost a let-down. This is not to say it lacks charm — on the contrary, the opening *Allegro* has plenty of vivacity and some delightful touches such a horn-like motif in the first subject group. (It is an arguable but interesting thought that while Haydn so often reminds one vividly in his sonatas of other instruments, I suspect it would be far easier to orchestrate those of Mozart.) There is much in this *Allegro* looking back to relatively archaic practices, including the ornate Rococo decoration surrounding the essentially simple opening theme (basically a much-embroidered broken chord). The sonata's greatest surprise comes at the close of the *Allegro*, when instead of repeating the second horn-call figure with which the codetta finished, the music comes to a sudden interrupted cadence on the dominant seventh and then plunges into a first inversion C sharp major chord for 21 bars of *Adagio*. This acts both as coda to the first movement and as replacement for a slow movement, and consists of a distinguished right-hand melody with a broken-chord accompaniment marked *staccatissimo* throughout. Even here there is no full close. Instead, after a cadence in E, the sonata goes without a break into the finale, once more in the tonic key. This is a formalised *Tempo di Menuet*, a series of six straightforward variations on a simple minuet tune, elegant and a trifle stiff. This formal experiment of writing a sonata without breaks between the movements is unique in Haydn's output, and the structural imbalance of the piece, as well as the plainness of many of its textures, make it perhaps one of the least satisfying of his mature works in the genre.

The E major work that follows, No. 46 (Hob. 31), also lacks a full slow movement. Here, we have an E minor *Allegretto* in strict three-part counterpoint throughout, as near an approach to a Bach Invention as there is in the sonatas, austerely moving and Baroque in feeling, ending with a cadence in B major and leading to the final *Presto* without a break. This time, the first movement is self-contained. The opening theme is a lovely melodic line, incorporating an equally beautiful and lyrical left-hand phrase:

Ex. 32(a) **Moderato**

Ex. 32(b)

I append here (Ex. 32(b)) my own suggestion for a more elaborate treatment of the right-hand part as an example of the kind of decoration one might wish to add if playing the repeats of both halves, because in performance this sonata presents the problem that, with two short but strongly marked movements following an expansive and essentially lyrical *Moderato*, one is really obliged to make all the repeats in the first movement so that the two halves of the sonata balance each other properly. However, to make all the *Moderato* repeats without substantially decorating it, and adding to or changing the ornamentation, would be to make it seem too long – it is in any case a joy to play twice! Essentially, all the melodic inspiration of the *Moderato* emanates from the idea of scales – Ex. 32(a) shows the top line descending and then ascending step-wise, and the sextuplets starting in bar 5 are also scales, with charming bass punctuations. A subsidiary idea in C sharp minor seems freer, but its main notes follow a similar outline to that of Ex. 32(a), and the second subject reverts to the sextuplet scales of bar 5, handled slightly differently and flowing more continuously but clearly related. The tone is intimate and gracious, and it is notable that halfway through the development, with a cadence on G sharp major and then a powerful C sharp minor enrichment of the second subject idea, the more dramatic and forceful potentialities of the material are revealed. There is a strong relationship between Ex. 32a and the main theme of the final *Presto*, emphasised on its third appearance by its restatement in thirds. This is a typical rondo-variation finale, with one episode in a virtuosic E minor before an extended and joyous final variation.

If the F major Sonata, No. 44, heralded a return to some of the *Sturm und Drang* techniques, the heightened passion of this world is more vividly recalled by the last sonata of this set, No. 47 in B minor (Hob. 32). This is the most emotionally powerful work since the C minor sonata, and though it lacks a slow movement it has great depth. The first movement, *Allegro moderato*, bases its opening theme on a series of inverted mordents, achieving particular vehemence in the development section. There are, as usual, a great many motivic ideas in this first subject group, of which a relatively light-hearted dotted rhythm becomes, in the development, the means whereby the music drives forward with great nervous energy to F sharp major and thence back to B minor for the recapitulation. The second subject starts with an imposing and richly scored passage:

Ex. 33

Allegro moderato

made even more darkly expressive in the recapitulation, both by being in B minor, the tonic key, and by major-key inflections in the flowing left-hand line adding a touch of expressive ambiguity. By way of relaxed contrast to this impassioned movement, the second is a perfectly poised Menuet, with one of the most long-breathed of Haydn's minuet tunes, though the B minor trio is more powerful and passionate, a contrast frequently encountered in such movements. After the Menuet has been repeated, Haydn takes us into one of the most surprising of all his finales, a *Presto* of demonic energy and ferocity. Were it not for the large number of pauses and rests, which as usual nearly always herald something of special importance, one might wish to describe it as a *moto perpetuo*, for it has all the atmosphere of an irresistible headlong flight. It is derived almost entirely from a figure starting, as a number of his finale themes do, with percussive repeated notes. This receives a variety of transformations, breaking out into circling semiquavers in the second subject group and receiving some strict contrapuntal treatment in the fiery development. As in the C minor Sonata, this is an unrelenting as well as an exciting movement, and it never lets up – it finishes with as uncompromising a gesture as one can imagine:

Ex. 34

The Middle Period: (iv) L. 48–57

Though the two sets of sonatas discussed above contain fine works, there can be little doubt that the second group is the finer, with at least three and possibly four masterpieces. Haydn's sonata writing has reached a high level both of adventurousness and of the ability to synthesise new and old elements into a coherent overall style. It is a curious coincidence, therefore, that after the B minor work, just as following the C minor Sonata earlier, he should produce a series of more modest pieces of quite startling inconsistency (in this respect he is not unlike Thomas Hardy, whose output of novels shows a similarly uneven achievement). Another coincidence is that it was the C minor that was added to Nos. 48–52 to make up this next set of six published in 1780 by Artaria as Op. 30 – the first Haydn works published by him, and the start of their long collaboration. Haydn himself correctly described the C minor as 'the longest and most difficult' of the set, and dedicated the six to Franziska and Marianne von Auenbrugger, the daughters of a well-respected medical man. They were known as excellent pianists, so it is surprising that the new sonatas, written during 1777–80, are not more demanding – they have their difficulties, of course, but on the whole they are less taxing than the previous set.

This is particularly true of the first, No. 48 in C (Hob. 35). A tiresome piece, it was for a long time one of the very few Haydn sonatas to achieve any place in the repertoire, possibly because it has the simplicity of a teaching piece, possibly also because its first movement, *Allegro con brio*, sounds more like Mozart than most of the others (Mozart on an off-day, I hasten to add) – it is certainly not Mozartean in its procedures, but the atmosphere is unusually near that of the younger man's lighter sonatas. This *Allegro* has 170 bars – in almost 100 of them an Alberti bass chunters along with very little else happening. This alone indicates the poverty of the ideas, which are simple and over-extended. There are plenty of typical touches, such as a fanfare-figure, a startling change of key almost as soon as the development has started (nullified by the banality of what follows), and several (perhaps too many) cadential pauses requiring embellishment, but none of these can lift the music on to a higher plane. It is sad that it must have given so many people their only exposure to Haydn sonatas – it is equally sad that, so far as I know, it was the only one recorded by Solomon. If only he had advocated some of the better ones! To be sure, matters are improved by a slow movement that is bigger and finer (with a second section obeying the basic sonata-form tonal habits while being simply a developed repeat of the first rather than a true development and recapitulation), but this too is over-long and contains too much of the ubiquitous Alberti bass. The best movement is the finale, a perky little rondo which is extremely simple. We have already had too much of this kind of simplicity in the sonata for this to be fully effective, but at least its proportions are right.

The C sharp minor Sonata which comes next, No. 49 (Hob. 36), is far better, possessing a magnificent first movement. For public performance, the work presents the problem that the second and third movements together hardly provide sufficient weight to balance the impact of the first – judgement of the tempo of the final Menuet becomes crucial here, for whilst it sounds superbly like a dramatic scherzo if taken quickly, a slower tempo enables it the better to balance the work as a whole. But it is the first movement, a powerful and concentrated *Moderato*, that dominates the work – dominates the whole set, indeed, if one excepts the C minor as being extraneous. The very key itself, C sharp minor, is a true *Sturm und Drang* tonality. The first subject governs all the thematic material, save for a lighter-textured codetta figure including a typical dotted rhythm – the opening phrase, transforming a Rococo turn into a dramatic gesture and containing characteristic repeated notes, contains the *Moderato*'s essence:

Ex. 35

The texture produced by the octave doublings in the first bar is an important part of the depth of sound in this movement, and though the second subject is largely an E major variant of the first, it is the minor key drama that dominates. A feature of this set of sonatas was that Haydn drew attention in his foreword to the publication to his use of the same theme in two different works, the first movement of No. 52 in G and the second movement (*Scherzando*) here. As an example of two different sets of variations on the same material it makes an interesting comparison, though William Newman has been so unkind as to suggest that it *might* simply have been a coincidence due to Haydn's inconsistent memory and his foreword merely a cover-up (as if a composer would ever do such a thing . . .). As it happens, in this sonata this *Allegro con brio* makes a charming and simple set of variations alternating major and minor keys, but it is not quite the impressive piece one might expect after such an outstanding first movement, and the real force of the sonata is resumed only in the finale, the Menuet referred to earlier. Its opening theme, which like the first subject of the *Moderato* begins with a written-out turn, is taken from a folk-tune, greatly transformed, and it is a most impressive, even Beethovenian piece, brief though it is – the lovely trio (in C sharp major!) has an almost Schubertian subtlety of lyrical grace, even a momentary hint of the *ländler*.

The D major Sonata which follows, No. 50 (Hob. 37), is, like the C major, one of the few to have become popular over the years, with more justification here, for, though not a particularly long work, it has sustained liveliness and character. The *Allegro con brio* with which it opens starts with a splendidly Handelian ring – this is music of unbuttoned amiability and yet power. The development section is quite short, but a descending chain of suspensions in the right hand over an ascending counter-subject in the left derived from the second subject group gives it all the authority it needs, and the movement as a whole retains a certain modesty of proportions despite its grandeur. It enables the two remaining movements, for all their brevity, to balance the first properly. The *Largo e sostenuto* is a sonorous, thoroughly Handelian sarabande in which Hungarian melodic traits have been noted, leading without a break to the bright, cheerful finale, a *Presto, ma non troppo* marked (aptly and characteristically) *innocentemente*. It is worth noting that the theme of this delightful finale covers two octaves, even in its first eight-bar phrase: compare this to the first theme of the *Allegro con brio*, which is contained within one octave and generally repeats or circles only a few notes. The variety of Haydn's melodic outlines is constantly inventive.

There is considerable similarity between this D major Sonata and No. 51 in E flat (Hob. 38), both in length and in overall shape – here too the slow movement leads directly to the finale. But the latter, a pleasantly decisive *Allegro* (actually a sort of minuet) with a lyrical A flat major section, is neither large enough nor sufficient of a resolution to the fine, siciliano-like *Adagio* for it to sustain the task of bringing the work to a real conclusion. The *Adagio* itself, however, has a Beethovian gravity and a deep sense of tragedy. It is in C minor and, interestingly, the first section, instead of having merely a repeat mark, is for once written out in full a second time, with extra ornamentation. It gives a good clue to the kind of embellishment Haydn might have anticipated in repeated sections:

Ex. 36(a)

Ex. 36(b)

As in earlier E flat sonatas, Haydn seems in the opening *Allegro moderato* to be anticipating his last in this key – this time with an astonishing number of ideas looking forward to that great work. This is a splendid movement, with a wealth of germinal motifs of many characteristic types and a fine air of spaciousness and serious wit. Once again, the development contains the most contrapuntal writing, and it is interesting in the exposition that the second subject group starts with a version in the dominant of the opening of the first group (initially an exact repetition), so that one hears it as a continuous flow. Again in the dominant, a striking new idea based on broken chords leaping upwards in the right hand takes the attention more dramatically, and it is here that one senses a new subject to be starting, even though it has actually been under way for six bars.

In the last sonata of the set, the G major No. 52 (Hob. 39), Haydn departs from his normal practice so far and gives the opening *Allegro con brio* the rondo-variation form, instead of leaving this structure to later in the work. The theme is the *scherzando* tune used also in the C sharp minor Sonata, but here it, is more inventively varied, and the couplets between the variations are more exciting – a delicately-turned one in G minor which is in fact a variation of the theme, and a rumbustious E minor episode derived from a dotted rhythm in the tune and turning into a lively 'Gypsy Rondo' sort of passage. The central movement is even better, an elaborate C major arioso marked *Adagio* – its expansive decorativeness and many details of texture and harmonic change are strongly anticipatory of the slow movement of Beethoven's G major Sonata, Op. 31 No. 1. The first section is repeated, but Haydn gives us first- and second-time bars, to enable a change to G minor for the development to proceed fluently after the repeat. The final *Prestissimo* is a scintillating sonata-form evoking to an exceptional degree the ghost of Scarlatti – its nimble opening theme consists simply of an octave leap and a written-out mordent in the right hand, with bass punctuation, until it breaks out into an octave scale and a turn-like motif. The high spirits are maintained to the end, but Haydn deftly turns away at the close with a delightfully simple, almost off-hand phrase in plain octaves – a typically witty conclusion.

After these three sets, Haydn's sonata output became intermittent until the group of three written for London in 1794/95. The reasons for this stem mainly, one supposes, from his pre-occupation with opera composition, which occupied him a great deal during the late 1770s and the 1780s.[1] The E minor Sonata, No. 53 (Hob. 34), was published first in London along with Nos. 34 and 35 in 1783/84, and, as is the case elsewhere (see No. 48 above), it is one of the few to have been frequently performed and taught over the years – a pity, because though it has a fine first movement, the second and third match it neither in quality of invention nor stature. The *Presto* (an exceptionally fast marking for a first movement, and in my view too fast – a really quick performance can miss the essentially symphonic nature of the piece) derives from the opening motif, an upward E minor arpeggio in the left hand followed by a three-note cadential tag in the right. The metre is 6/8, something only encountered once before in his sonata first movements (No. 19, also in E minor), and only encountered once more (the very next sonata, in G major – the relative major), and Haydn exploits to the full the contrast between the comfortable lilt of this metre and the toughness of the actual material – the movement has a marvellous strength and coherence and at the same time an ambiguity that enhances its dark edge. The G major *Adagio* that follows has an aria-like melodic warmth at the start, but it soon breaks into florid arabesques that all but over-balance it in the direction of over-elaboration of essentially simple ideas – there is, however, a dramatic interruption at the close in the form of an extended cadence moving the music towards E minor for the final *Vivace molto*, which follows without a break. Doubtless it was this rondo that gave the work its popularity, for it has a charming little tune, some pleasant touches of humour, and some degree of variation (the episodes them-selves are variants of the main theme, in E major) – but there is hardly enough variety to sustain interest, and the Alberti bass is once more revealed as a sign of weakness. One is tempted to suspect that the finales of both this and No. 48 probably gave rise to the popularity of those works solely because they fit in so perfectly with the misguided but still, sadly, prevalent view of Haydn as little more than an amiable funster.

The three short (two-movement) sonatas that follow, dedicated to Princess Marie Esterházy, were published in 1784, the year after her marriage to Prince Nicolaus. (Arrangements for String trio were published by Hoffmeister in 1788, but it seems likely that the piano versions were the originals.) They have sometimes been dismissed as

---

1 The operas written between 1770–91 are *L'infedeltà delusa*, *L'incontro improvviso*, *Il mondo della luna*, *La vera costanza*, *L'isola disabitata*, *La fedeltà premiata*, *Orlando Paladino*, *Armida*, and *L'anima del filosofo*. In addition, the 1780s saw the composition of 19 string quartets (the sets Opp. 33, 50, 54 and 55, plus Op. 42 in D minor) as well as the *Seven Last Words* in their quartet version – the six quartets of Op. 64 followed in 1790.

trivial. To overlook the very real qualities of invention and work-manship of these charming little pieces would be foolish, however. They rely very much on variation and/or rondo forms for their structures – only the middle work, No. 55 in B flat (Hob. 41), has a full sonata form, the opening *Allegro*. This splendid movement is driven forward by the dotted rhythm of its imposing and vigorous opening phrase, and though the Alberti bass appears during the second subject group, it is used with discretion and skill. It is a genuinely large-scale movement in impact, and the tightly organised *Allegro di molto* that follows balances it well, making up in motivic concentration and little touches of en-riching counterpoint what it lacks in length.

Sonata No. 56 in D (Hob. 42) is the only one of this group to have a slow movement, the opening *Andante con espressione* (Haydn's tempo markings are becoming a shade more explicit). This is a large-scale set of increasingly elaborate and resourceful variations on a simple, rather hesitant theme – it is interesting to compare it with the first movement of the C major Sonata, No. 58, written a few years later. The tempo marking is the same, and both theme and variations, as in No. 56, are full of pauses or rests – indeed, both movements are supreme examples of Haydn's skill, noted before, at using silence as an integral part of the music. If the later *Andante* is the more impressive, that of No. 56 is hardly far behind it in richness or imagination. The finale of this sonata derives its sinuous, chromatically inflected main theme from a left-hand phrase in the accompaniment at the end of the *Andante*'s theme, first part – this *Vivace assai* is a cunningly worked little piece, really an exploration of two motifs from its main theme rather than either a true rondo or true variation form. Its intricacy is delightful, and belies its superficial charm.

But my own personal favourite of these three lovely works is the first, No. 54 in G (Hob. 40). The delightfully lilting variations of the opening *Allegretto innocente* are as full of clever little inflections of harmony or rhythm as any movement in this set, and within its fairly short span it covers an extraordinarily wide range of detail. The powerfully witty *Presto* which follows is a particularly clear example of Haydn's love of third-related keys. The first part of the ritornello section is in G, ending in the dominant – the second begins abruptly in B flat, ending in the tonic once more. The episode succeeding this is in E minor – its dramatic intensity is a perfect foil for the high spirits of the ritornello, which returns to control the rest of the movement with some joyous decoration and development. For all its brevity, it is a wonderful little piece.

In 1788 Artaria issued a mixed collection of keyboard works including the Sonata No. 57 in F (Hob. 47), which takes the first two movements of the E minor Sonata No. 19 discussed earlier, transposes them up a semitone and places them second and third, adding a new first movement to make up the work. Doubts have been cast on the authenticity of this first movement, but there now seems little doubt that it is indeed by Haydn. It is a flowing two-part invention for the most part, the right hand breaking into thirds and octaves only towards the end of each half. Harold Truscott, in the Penguin anthology *The Symphony* (1966), has pointed out the resemblance between the opening theme of this *Moderato* and that of Bach's F major *English Suite*, and it is a distinctly Bachian movement, though without the richness Bach supplies. Oddly enough, the sound of the music is not unlike that of the contrapuntal writing in Mozart's *Allegro* in F, the first movement of that wonderful hybrid work K. 533/494, but it lacks the same concentration as well as the inventive variety that Haydn normally commands. The siciliano second movement, now marked *Larghetto* instead of *Adagio*, is as fine and moving as before – there are only a few changes of tiny details, and the same is true of the lively *Allegro* into which it goes without a break. Why Haydn chose to resurrect an earlier work in this way is not known – but in any event, uneven though the sonata is, the *Allegro* works better as a finale than as a middle movement, its placing in the original version.

The Late Period: (i) L. 58 and 59

The *Andante con espressione* variations opening the C major Sonata, No. 58 (Hob. 48), have already been noted in connection with Sonata No. 56 above. The work appeared in 1789 in a *Musikalisches Pot-pourri* ('little musical vegetable pot', as Haydn described it) published by Breitkopf, who had asked him to write something specially for him. Though the other five sonatas requested by Breitkopf never materialised, he had reason to be pleased with this one. After a period in which Haydn's interest in sonatas seems to have been waning (Nos. 54–56 are inspired but miniature and the others are, to say the least, inconsistent), it is good to find his genius working at full stretch again. His love of the alternating major/minor variation form achieves its summation in the first movement and the new influence of Clementi's powerful keyboard style, which Haydn is known rightly to have admired, is integrated into his own finale-rondo type for the only other movement, somewhat optimistically marked *Presto*. The *Andante*, for which *Adagio* would be a marking more in keeping with the music's immense gravity, is by far the most richly scored piece Haydn has thus far produced for keyboard – it exploits to the full the tonal characteristics of each register of the instrument, and the dynamic markings, exceptionally detailed and careful, testify to his concern to be as explicit as possible. Even at a slow pace, there is something mercurial as well as serious about some of the changes of texture and key – it is a superbly sustained movement, greatly challenging the performer to maintain the tension through a large number of silences (this is perhaps the apotheosis of this aspect of his keyboard work). The variations develop from the start, even in the first four bars, of which 3 and 4 are already an intensification of 1 and 2:

Ex. 37

Andante con espressione

The fantasia-like, but always unified, variety of treatments of the theme in both major and minor keys is astonishing. No less remarkable is the finale, by far the most symphonic of Haydn's keyboard rondos to date, as much in the complexity of the argument than in the weight of sound produced by the influence of Clementi:

Ex. 38

Even the rondo theme itself, a motif of which can be seen in Ex. 38 from the beginning of the first episode, is more akin to his orchestral rondo tunes than anything previous in the keyboard works. It makes a resounding conclusion, and expands the resources at his command with great assurance.

Perhaps because it has only two movements, this work is not heard as often as it deserves. Its successor, the masterly E flat Sonata No. 59 (Hob. 49), has, however, established itself quite firmly in the repertoire – deservedly, since in quality and depth it yields nothing to the last three sonatas still to come. Behind the dedication there is an amusing story, for Haydn promised the work to two different ladies (who were, however, friends). It was commissioned by Maria Anna Jerlischek, who married the violinist Jean Tost (to whom Haydn dedicated his Op. 64 Quartets) in about 1790, the year the sonata was completed. But Haydn also promised it to his close friend Marianne von Genzinger. As it happens, the first and third movements had been composed either in 1788 or 1789 – it was the central slow movement, which he told Marianne was 'full of significance', that was written in 1790 at a time when he was lonely and troubled. It is well known that Marianne was an excellent pianist, though she did ask Haydn, unavailingly, to simplify the crossed-hands passage in the slow movement.

It is obvious from the start of the first movement that there is a special vigour and concentration about the music, both in the intensely motivic nature of the melodic line and in the full-bodied thirds which punctuate it in the left hand and give it its springy impulse:

Ex. 39(a)

Ex. 39(b)

Ex. 39(a) gives the first four bars, Ex. 39(b) the first five bars of the second subject group, in which the motifs marked *x* and *y* have now been extended and developed – underneath *y* in the latter there is an Alberti bass, but it should be stressed that, far from being simply a formula, this device is now used with the utmost creativity to keep the music flowing forward and to lead to the harmonic changes with marvellously natural effect. The dotted rhythm at the end of Ex. 39(a) plays only a small part in the movement, such is the wealth of imaginative treatment and concentration Haydn obtains from this opening phrase, so simple and so full of potential. For the substantial closing section, motif *y* provides the main material, leading to an interrupted cadence, a rest, and then, transforming the rhythm ♩♩♩ | ♩ which begins *y* by means of repeated notes, into an uncanny and quiet 'pre-echo' of the 'fate' motif from Beethoven's Fifth Symphony. It has an even closer relationship, in its effect though to a different metre, with the first movement of the same composer's *Appassionata* sonata, as a lengthy and mysterious passage towards the end of the development makes clear – indeed, these two works make an excellent pair for the first half of a recital if one feels strong enough to tackle them together! This passage, indeed, is so remarkable that it demands further investigation, for after the mysterious part just mentioned, Haydn then gives us a rich passage of polyphony leading to an emphatic reiteration of the 'fate' rhythm. There follows a transition in which, with the bass moving down from B natural to B flat, it is combined with the opening right-hand phrase of motif *x* rising from the bass clef to a top F and, after a pause, there is a cadenza-like scale curling down to return us to the recapitulation proper. It is a marvellously sustained and imaginative section, with its mystery finally broken by the bass moving to the dominant note and the anticipations of the first subject taking us naturally back to its full restatement, and it typifies the magnificently symphonic growth of the work. Even when the coda is reached Haydn finds exciting new possibilities in the material.

The *Adagio e cantabile* is wonderfully expressive and complex. Basically it has three sections: (i) a lengthy B flat major one starting with a theme clearly related to motif *y* from Ex. 39(a) and containing a large number of other important and inter-related ideas; (ii) a more passionate central section in B flat minor and then D flat major marked by the notorious crossed-hands passage and then a great lyrical flowering; and (iii) a return to the B flat major part, slightly condensed and elaborately decorated. The opening theme itself, in fact, makes four reappearances during the course of the movement, each time varied and sometimes elaborated quite ornately by wreathing decoration – but it is not the kind of Rococo arabesquerie that served to 'fill in the gaps' or make repetition less wearisome in some of the weaker earlier sonatas, but rather a type which looks forward to the Romantic era, enhancing and springing directly from the expressive needs of the music. The scoring for the instrument in this movement is remarkable for its subtlety and strength – more than anything, I am reminded of the wonderful slow movement of the F major Sonata No. 44, the only one previously to breathe quite so precisely the profound, maturely Classical air of this one, and the difference in the subtlety of the design and its complex working-out shows how far Haydn had matured in the intervening years (which is not to belittle the earlier piece).

The finale is simpler, the apotheosis of his decorated minuet style — marked *Tempo di Menuet*, it is a generous example of its kind, thematically another reworking of the motifs from Ex. 39(a). The trio is, like the minuet, in E flat major, and the minuet's reappearance is marked by a shift to E flat minor after the first phrase; there is a degree of development before the return of the tonic major and a final, more triumphant restatement of the main theme. It is a charming and mellifluous movement, both intimate and sufficiently large-scale to make an admirable conclusion to this masterwork. Those who regard only the three 'London' sonatas as the peak of Haydn's output in this genre make a sad error of judgement if they regard this work as in any way inferior.

The Late Period: (ii) The Last Three Sonatas

There is a marked difference between the style of piano writing of No. 59 and that of the last three sonatas, an added degree of orchestral power. There are several possible contributory causes. One is Haydn's great ability to respond with unfailing intellectual vigour to the stimulus afforded by the flourishing pianistic environment in London. Another is that whereas No. 59 was written for an excellent amateur performer, the last three were for the distinguished concert pianist Therese Jansen, at whose wedding to the engraver Bartolozzi Haydn was a witness. A third is that he had access to newer and more powerful instruments – Marianne von Genzinger herself did not even own a fortepiano in 1790 – and the influence of these new instruments can be felt as surely in the accompaniments to his English Canzonets (especially such songs as the *Sailor's Song*) as in these sonatas. The three works were written in 1794/95, and there has been some doubt about their order of composition (and, indeed, whether the short D major Sonata, No. 61, was really intended for Therese Jansen) – the evidence is conflicting, but since the E flat is such a supreme crown to the corpus of Haydn's sonatas it makes good sense to regard it as the last. (It is worth adding that his last three piano trios, those in C, E and E flat were also written for Therese Jansen, probably in 1796, and mark the pinnacle of his achievement in that genre.) Oddly enough, it is the C major Sonata, No. 60 (Hob. 50), that takes the keyboard range to its highest extreme, up to a top A, which was not to appear in Beethoven's sonatas until the *Waldstein* of 1803/04.

If the opening movement of the Marianne von Genzinger Sonata in E flat (No. 59) was a superb exhibition of concentrated motivic working, the first *Allegro* of this C major Sonata is even more an intellectual triumph, a complex web of thematic inter-relationships and at the same time an invigorating and virtuosic symphonic first movement:

Ex. 40

This apparently simple, almost skeletal first subject contains, as the example shows, a large number of suggestive motifs and, in the gradual slowing-down by means of a pause in bar 6 followed by the renewed, self-confident assertion of the subject in its pomp, an ebb and flow of tension giving a kind of ambiguity between increasing hesitancy and rediscovered assertiveness to occur frequently in this movement – the whole passage leading back from the body of the development to the recapitulation is a superb decoration of this little idea on a much larger scale, involving not only dissolution of the texture followed by a new enrichment of it as the music seems to have found the right path again (a process undergone several times) but also a careful handling of tonality so that the dominant seventh chord preceding the recapitulation is seen in the end as the result of a tonal search which has been going on for some time. The dominant seventh itself is asserted *fortissimo* with thick chords in both hands, a moment of triumphant arrival, a fanfare to herald the return of the first subject – which, however, is once again modest and *piano* just as at the start, a wonderfully witty touch which would be ruined if the performer were ever so misguided as to decorate the three beats of rest after the dominant seventh chord to fill in the silence. (It occurs to me that one of the reasons for the neglect of Haydn's sonatas might be his use of silence, since most soloists seem terrified that if they observe all the rests, even in Chopin, the audience will go to sleep.)

But back to the first subject itself. It is no surprise that it also provides the second subject material, in bar 20, the theme heard in strong left-hand octaves against a scalic right-hand passage – it is interesting that the scale goes upwards as the left hand descends so that the hands are moving in contrary motion, a precise inversion of the process in bar 7 of Ex. 40 above, where the three chords move inwards. The various motifs of Ex. 40 provide other relevant ideas – for instance, the sevenths (motif v) are significant, and the left-hand accompanying figure z is important in the closing sections of exposition and recapitulation and especially in the development, where another idea links it with v. In the part leading up to the second subject group, Haydn combines the shape of the left-hand phrase y from bar 9 with the all-important thirds from w, placing the resulting theme above a varied version of the left-hand octave leap x to give us a cadential idea which is again given an extra dimension during the second subject group by subtle alteration:

Ex. 41

(The little tag in the bass clef from bar 19 is brilliantly used as part of the section finding its way back to the recapitulation discussed above.) I cannot resist quoting from this scintillating movement a passage of most extraordinary, almost Wagnerian chromaticism. It occurs in all three parts of the movement – here is its powerful appearance in the development, showing the wide range of tonalities encompassed in this remarkable work by starting in B (itself reached by a cunning side-step) and ending, via a most exotic route, in E major:

Ex. 42

It hardly needs to be pointed out that the bass accompaniment is *not* simply an accompanying figure but derives initially from motif *x* in Ex. 40! Along with the tonal excursions typified by this example, Haydn takes the opportunity in the development (and elsewhere) to show his mastery of the integration of closely-woven counterpoint into his sonata structure:

Ex. 43

There are those who consider this *Allegro* austere or intellectual. Certainly it has astounding intellectual qualities, but its combined wit and sobriety, bravura brilliance and subtle expressiveness make it for me music of real exultation. Even the simple beginning, the music seeming to lose its way and then re-asserting itself with a new sense of purpose (even the feeling of a new, perhaps a 'real' beginning after a false start) and at the same time a development of ideas implicit in the opening bars, has an exciting quality of life-giving energy.

The *Adagio* was published in a slightly different version by Artaria of Vienna in 1794, so it is known that the sonata was begun before Haydn had even left on his second London trip. (For some inexplicable reason, it is his only sonata to have been given a nickname, *The English* – any one of the three could be so called, and, since nicknames are such an aid to identification, I regret the lack of any more.) This is a dignified sonata form, with a fairly short development section and no real second subject group but rather a clearly identified new theme in the tonic which makes the contrast normally to be expected of a 'textbook' second subject. The dominant key is reached only for the codetta. The warm resonance of this fine movement is subtly enhanced by contrapuntal and chromatic touches, and though the thematic ideas themselves are mostly new, there are some hidden references to some of the germinal motifs from the *Allegro* (notably *w* and *y* from Ex. 40, the right-hand thirds from Ex. 41, and the contrapuntal writing as shown in Ex. 43).

The final *Allegro molto* is a scherzo – the derivation from minuet style can be demonstrated by playing the main theme at a normal, steady minuet pace. It is bi-partite, with the repeat of each 'half' written out. The first section, opening with a tune closely akin to that of the C major Fantasia of 1789, repeats the device from the first movement of pausing as if the composer has lost his way, and this trick, usually suggesting the imminent arrival of a key which would distort the tonal scheme, gives much humour to the second part. Here, after a variant of the first section has expanded the key scheme, it is repeated more powerfully and full-bloodedly, with some extra development of the hesitation/assertion trick. It is all done with such energy that the repetition of this part merely whets one's appetite to hear the whole thing again. Typically, Haydn brings the sonata to a gentle, *piano* close, deftly and wittily bringing a powerful and complex work to a delicious conclusion.

The little D major Sonata, No. 61 (Hob. 51), is totally different to any other in Haydn's output. Instead of the massive symphonic style of the works flanking it, the two movements inhabit an intimate and charming world. The opening *Andante* is formally simple, a single section containing several melodic ideas, the second subject group starting in the dominant with a variant of the first theme and also providing a rhythmic idea for the codetta. A couple of bars modulate back to the tonic and the section is repeated, the tunes varied in both detail and order of appearance, and then, after modulating to the dominant, there is a return to the tonic and a third, shorter version of the same section. The central part is often thought of as a development, but it seems to me simply an altered reprise of the first section, while the third part is thus an extra reprise instead of a formal recapitulation. It is mellifluous, flowing music, with many touches subsequently associated with Schubert – the accompanying triplets going through much of it anticipate the finale of Schubert's late A major Sonata, D. 959, especially when placed under a staccato theme in crotchets, and there could hardly be anything more evocative of Schubert (who was not yet born!) than the B flats in the closing cadence:[1]

Ex. 44

1 Jerald C. Graue has pointed out that this, and many other details, owe much to the example of Dussek (in *Haydn Studies*, ed. Larsen, Serwer and Webster, 1981, New York and London.

The finale, marked *Presto*, has the same form as the finale of the C major Sonata, though here it is only the repeat of the second, larger section that is written-out. Another scherzo in style, it has an extraordinary number of off-beat *sforzandi* and accents, akin to Beethoven at his most unbuttonedly humorous. The keyboard writing itself owes much to Clementi – it should be recalled that Clementi and Haydn were present together in London and took part in public concerts either in collaboration or competition. Undoubtedly Haydn's expanded keyboard style derives as much from Clementi's example as from the new, bigger instruments at his disposal. It is startling to think that some good authorities regarded this work, which could almost be early nineteenth-century, as being earlier than it actually is!

The classical structure of sonata form incorporated as its lynch-pin the dramatic·idea of the opposition of two types, or characters, represented by the first and second subjects (often characterised as 'masculine' and 'feminine'). It is this dialogue, antagonism, or confrontation that gives rise to the essential idea of the development section, in which the two elements explore their identities, and then the recapitulation, in which, by placing both themes in the tonic, there is an air of resolution about the drama. For Haydn, as later for Schubert, sonata form was something else, the basis for an exploration of the first subject group material. There are many sonatas with clearly differentiated second subjects – there are others where there are three different subject areas, the codetta becoming as important as the others, while the 'expansion' sections which have sometimes dovetailed with and sometimes replaced a formal second subject group make yet another area for variation and extension. But his most typical approach to the form is encountered in the C major and E flat major sonatas under discussion, where the thematic material is almost entirely derived from one cell or group of cells – the contrasting character given by its treatment as a second subject is all the 'character drama' Haydn needs, the dialogue being not a juxtaposition of opposing types but a dramatic examination of one.

In no other sonata does he explore the ramifications of tonal relationships so profoundly as in these two works, especially the E flat Sonata, No. 62 (Hob. 52), where his handling of sonata form is both closely akin to that of the C major Sonata, and subtly different. Here there is an added sense of freedom – the working-out of the motifs is less rigorous, though no less complex, and the harmonic and tonal richness if anything even more striking. The massive opening, a powerful statement of intent in a markedly 'public' manner, contains a multitude of ideas:

Ex. 45

Apart from the motifs *w*, *x*, *y* and *z* one should note the dotted rhythm in the right hand (bar 1), with its clear relationship to the rhythm of the more chromatic tune in bar 6 *et seq.*, and the left-hand accompanying figure in bar 6, which is developed into a more melodic counter-subject in later versions of this phrase, either above the melody line or below it. The second subject group contains two distinct phases, the first a tremendous expansion of the range of bars 1 and 2:

Ex. 46

This introduces into the texture, by extending the figure *x*, the virtuosic scale passages that are to be such a feature of this technically demanding movement and which recur in the finale's development. The other main idea of the second-subject group sounds more like the contrasting theme one expects in conventional sonata form, again (like Ex. 46) in the dominant – but one can detect a link with the thirds of motif *y*, the influence of the first theme's dotted rhythms, and, by the introduction of chromaticisms which inflect the music by implying the lurking presence of more distant keys, the figure *z*:

Ex. 47

In Exx. 45 and 47 one can already see how Haydn's masterly handling of tonality adds to the solidity of the movement a touch of mercurial ambiguity with the move to a first inversion of A flat in bar 6 (Ex. 45) enlarging the tonal horizons at an early stage, and the shift to B flat minor at the end of Ex. 47 adding a darker colouring to the brilliant textures (something already suggested by the implied imminence of B flat minor before Ex. 46 bursts out in the major key). Haydn exploits these subtle contrasts, and the rich opportunities for 'orchestration', by using different registers of the piano (the horn-like tune in the left hand of Ex. 47 emphasises his notably orchestral style). The codetta ends with a brassy flourish, and starts with a third version of bars 1 and 2, commencing with three chords moving in contrary motion:

Ex. 48

It should be stressed that the variety of tonal implications produced by the chromatic passing notes in the exposition do not have an unsettling effect – Haydn underpins it with the massive solidity of the overall tonal planning, a substantial portion being based on the tonic key and then, with Ex. 46 starting the second subject, remaining on or near the dominant for the remainder of this section. Only two bare and mysterious octaves in the middle of the codetta, before the final flourish, suggest other latent forces.

The dramatic changes of key in the development create a thoroughly intricate web of interlocking key relationships. Starting on the dominant, a simple, quiet cadence leads to a pause on G major, the mediant of E flat – in his A flat Sonata, Op. 110, Beethoven uses a similar, equally effective device to move into the first movement's development. Ex. 47, now in C major, starts to develop and moves gradually through F, D, G minor and C minor to an emphatic, virtuosic A flat (which, however, is revealed a few bars later as merely a step on the way to G major, a key emphasised by powerful flourishes alternating between G and its subdominant minor, C). Before long there is another pause on a G major chord, both hands in the bass, and suddenly, with a great wrench to E major, Ex. 47 is reworked. By way of an extended treatment of motif z, the tonic is gradually neared for the recapitulation to begin. The almost bewildering diversity of motifs, textures and, above all, keys in this wonderful development is fascinating, but one senses that despite its fantastic freedom it is immensely purposeful, and so it proves. The slow movement is to be in E major, the flattened supertonic of the work's tonic key and a most bold choice for the period (Beethoven created a similar kind of aural shock by also placing in E major the slow movement of his C minor piano concerto) – by making the presence of the key of E so strongly felt in the middle of the movement Haydn draws our attention to it and so reinforces the tonal scheme of the whole work, just as in the slow movement he gives us an E minor middle section emphasising its relative major, G, which in turn is the mediant of E flat major, the key of the finale. One more characteristic of these relationships should be noted, and that is once again Haydn's love of third-related keys (the interval of a third underlies much of the melodic invention in the *Allegro*, too) – E flat or E major/minor to G, E major to A flat (G sharp, the third of E major, being enharmonically the same as A flat), and so on. By emphasising A flat so strongly seven bars before the shift to E major in the development he gives another, even more subconsciously appreciated, clue to his intentions – even the first inversion of A flat in bar 6 noted earlier can in retrospect be regarded as a hint of this large-scale tonal organisation, and it is not too far-fetched to suggest that in bar 1 itself the immediate shift from the tonic to first inversion subdominant is similarly intended.

Before the end of the *Allegro*, Haydn springs one more surprise by extending the two quiet double octaves from the codetta before the concluding flourish. This time he extends this phrase with the aid of a C flat and B double flats – enharmonically it could be written as a simple phrase in E major, and this would make clearer its importance as more preparation for the slow movement's key. Extraordinary key relationships were nothing new, of course – C. P. E. Bach himself employed them quite often. In his Sonata in G major, Wq. 56 No. 2, for example, he links the first movement to a slow movement *in C sharp minor* by a simple but shattering diminished chord coming like a bolt from the blue, and there are plenty of other examples, usually with some underlying preparation for the key change during the previous movement. But the calm authority and detailed planning of Haydn's procedures gives it a feeling of inevitability – techniques used to shock and surprise are now being employed to enrich and enlarge the expressive depths of the music. It is a wonderfully lively and joyous first movement, Jove-like in its grandeur rather than merely jovial.

In *The Sonata Principle: Man and his Music* (1957) Wilfred Mellers has aptly described some of the feeling and significance of this sonata: 'the drama is now resolved in a structure radiant with light. Apollonian order implies a new kind of belief. Haydn's God was not the mystical divinity of Bach, or the Lord of earthly glory of Handel; but all his later music is religious in the sense that it reflects the beliefs that had meaning for him – an ethical humanism based on reason and the love of created nature. The development of his own ostensibly religious music shows him gradually discovering, in ecclesiastical terms, the religion that is implicit in his later instrumental music.' This applies especially well to the central *Adagio*, imbued as it is with spiritual grace. It opens with a bi-partite section whose main theme, though it has some links with Ex. 45 (notably the descending thirds), has its own unique identity – it soars over a range of more than two octaves and as it reaches further and wider it increases in richness of scoring and dynamics until descending once more to a quiet cadence. The central part of the movement is almost entirely built out of the first three notes of the main theme, a true development first in E minor and then in G. There is an almost fantasia-like freedom about the decoration which the theme is given both in the exposition section (on its return at the end of the second half) and in the recapitulation, but it never disturbs the serenity of this lovely music, and the long final cadence, extended over a tonic pedal-note for four bars, has a sense of absolute peace and resolution.

As if to celebrate the state of grace that has been achieved, the finale, *Presto*, is a brilliant romp, simply the best of its kind in the sonatas, and yet quite complex. The first five notes, stuttering away on a repeated G (natural, cancelling at once the G sharp in the *Adagio*'s final chord), make a pivot to swing the tonality back to E flat, established beneath the sixth repeated G – how typical of Haydn at his finest to use a delightful and witty opening to achieve both entertainment and a formal purpose. After a few bars, the tune comes to a halt, and attempts to get under way in F minor with some repeated A flats in the right hand and the succeeding phrase also transposed up a tone – the pounding accompaniment in both cases is reminiscent of a peasant dance. Another pause follows, and then the left hand, with some *forte* repeated B flat octaves, puts a stop to all these shenanigans and gets the movement properly under way, the theme itself now remaining in the left hand and becoming, in effect, a bass line to the brilliantly virtuosic right-hand part. The repeated notes return in the codetta to drive the music onwards, and of course in the recapitulation (this is after all a sonata form in rondo style) the opening joke is repeated – it is a good one and never palls. The same figure opens the development and leads to a written-out *adagio* cadenza at its end via a chromatic, charmingly extended variant of the initial joke. Some rather Scarlattian figuration, extended in the development to powerful effect, and a warmly lyrical contrasting phrase (not substantial enough for a true second subject) make up the main elements in a movement that completes Haydn's sonata work in a spirit of untramelled delight.

Other Solo Keyboard Works

In the Christa Landon edition, three sonatas have been dropped from the canon, all of them included in Päsler/Hoboken. The C major Sonata, Hob. 15, is an inferior and dubious arrangement of three movements from the Divertimento in C (Hob. II/11), hardly worth attention. Hob. 16 is an oddly uneven work in E flat, of anonymous authorship (though certainly not by Haydn) – its second and third movements are charming, if a shade primitive, and the first has some interesting eccentricities, though hardly convincing even as a fantasia. No. 17 in B flat is now thought to be by J. G. Schwanenberg (or Schwanenberger) – it is decidedly un-Haydnesque, but its three movements have much charm. Apparently modelled on J. C. Bach's B flat major Sonata, Op. 17 No. 6, it is well worth investigation as a period piece.

It would be unjust to omit, from even so limited a survey as this, some description of Haydn's other keyboard works. Before doing so, however, I should like to make a plea for those who find the sonatas rewarding to turn their attention also to the piano trios. This marvellous corpus of works, like the sonatas, has suffered a comparable neglect, save for a few (again, not always the best). This may be partly due to the cello parts, which are regarded by many cellists as being thoroughly dispensable – which is simply untrue, as can be shown if one can persuade cellists to perform the works, when they realise that the cello lines are not only texturally essential but are in their way artistically challenging. There are, in Robbins Landon's edition (published in the *Diletto Musicale* series by Doblinger), 45 piano trios, and they cover a wide range of Haydn's career, the last ones post-dating the last sonatas. There are at least a dozen genuine masterpieces among them, and a knowledge of them adds immeasurably to one's understanding of Haydn's development as a keyboard composer.

Of the remaining works for solo keyboard, there are several sets of variations and a number of short pieces. Of the variations, those in D (Hob. XVII/7) appear also as the second movement of the piano trio in D (L. 15, omitted by Hoboken) – this is a fairly primitive work, the authenticity of which is still in doubt. Two charming sets are those in C (Hob. XVII/5) and E flat (Hob. XVII/3). The C major work is light and decorative, mostly set in the higher registers of the keyboard. They were written in 1790 for Artaria, with a view to being useful to amateurs, and they are given an extra degree of variety and character by fanfare-figures in the third variation and by the fifth being in the minor key. The final variation brings the set to a lively conclusion.

The so-called Arietta in E flat 'con 12 variazioni' is more graceful, the theme derived from the minuet of the string quartet, Op. 9 No. 2. There are subtly Mozartean touches of harmony here and there, and the work seems to have been immensely popular in its time. Franz Eibner, in the preface to his edition (published by Universal), suggests that since the final variation is a touch inconclusive, performers might like to repeat the tune to round the work off. It is a charming piece, less varied in texture and decoration perhaps than the C major variations, but worth attention nonetheless. There is also a larger set of Variations in G (Hob. XVII/2) or, in a later version with only 12 variations instead of the original 20, in A (Hob. XVII/8). This is more in the tradition of a chaconne than the others – the bass line is the same throughout, and above it Haydn explores a wide variety of treatments of a simple little theme. In a sense, it looks forward to Beethoven's 32 Variations in C minor, again derived from the chaconne, though this work of Haydn is thought to have been complete in both versions by 1770. Personally, I prefer the A major version, but both are exciting and florid, not unlike similar pieces by Handel in their powerful momentum and extrovert geniality.

Of the various short pieces, mostly slow, a simple but hauntingly beautiful *Adagio* in F (Hob. XVII/9) stands out – published in 1786, it is a lovely, serene piece, though whether an arrangement or shortened version of something else is not known. The Capriccio in G (Hob. XVII/1) is a different matter altogether: 368 bars long, it is a ritornello form in which the folksong *Acht Sauschneider müssen seyn* is varied considerably on its many reappearances. The Capriccio dates from the early 1760s, and one of its most remarkable features is the vast range of keys through which it passes, often related by thirds in the familiar way. Haydn's handling of the left-hand part is amazingly resourceful for such an early work and, though it is a difficult piece to programme in recital these days (the many repetitions can become wearisome), it repays close attention, not least for the light it throws on the strong influence of C. P. E. Bach on this type of rondo form.

But the two finest of Haydn's separate keyboard works remain the F minor Variations and the Fantasia in C major. The latter, a *Presto* in 3/8 time, dates from 1789 and is based on a theme later to be used for the finale of the C major Sonata No. 60 (*The English*). Formally, it is a kind of ecstatically free, rather eccentric rondo, in that while it is all derived from the main theme or an arpeggio figure following it, the organisation makes it *sound* like a ritornello structure – in its almost improvisatory freedom, it also shows the influence of C. P. E. Bach's fantasias, which were at the time firmly established models of their kind. Haydn's typical keyboard style, with its vivid recollections of other instrumental timbres (a horn-call phrase plays a vital cadential role in this piece), is as virtuosic as it ever was – this is, first and foremost, a vastly enjoyable display piece. But the apparent wildness of its freer passages is tightly controlled, and the frequent dramatic modulations make excellent tonal sense – they are, not surprisingly, often between third-related keys (a pause on D major and then an outburst in B flat, for instance, or a move soon afterwards from E major back to the tonic C for the ritornello theme). It makes an admirable recital piece in its own right, as well as an apt partner for *The English* Sonata, and it is odd that our virtuosi have not made it into a warhorse by now.

The F minor Variations, however, have become standard repertoire, though it is surprising that their depth of expression has often been regarded as something of a 'sport' in Haydn's output, rather than something characteristic. The tone of the work is melancholy, nostalgic even, rather than passionate, until in the extensive coda it suddenly breaks out into one of the most powerful tragic outbursts in piano music (the more powerful, of course, by coming at the end of such an intimate and restrained work), leading to a conclusion that is the distillation of bleakness and emotional loss. (The sense of emptiness is emphasised by the open fifth marked *x*, a perfect instance of Haydn's use of instrumental colouring to enhance the feeling of the music, and something

Ex. 49

going back to the open fifth which concludes his *Sturm und Drang*
Symphony No. 44 in E minor, *The Trauer*). The Variations were
written in 1793 for Barbara von Ployer, a well-known pianist for whom
Mozart wrote his concerti K. 449 and K. 453, and they were given
three different titles: Sonata (the autograph manuscript), *Un piccolo
Divertimento* (a manuscript copy by his copyist Elssler), and *Variations
pour le Clavecin ou Piano-Forte* (Artaria's first edition). Nowadays, they
tend to be known as either *Andante con variazioni* or simply Variations in
F minor. The form is a typical alternating variation structure with the
bi-partite first theme in F minor and the second, also in two halves, in F
major – the two are less closely related and rather more complementary
than usual. The themes themselves are most beautiful, the first especially so (the dotted rhythms pervading it give it an extraordinary
combination of rhythmic lift and added sadness), and the two variations
on each are extensively decorative but inspired and subtle. After the
second major key variation, Haydn originally added a few bars of F
major flourish to close the work – had he not changed his mind and
given us the magnificent coda we now have, the work would surely have
been far less significant. It is not certain what caused him to add the
coda, which starts like a reprise of the opening theme and quite
suddenly veers off into a new world, but there is no doubt that he was
deeply affected by the death of Marianne von Genzinger in January 1793
and it seems likely that this loss affected the passionate conclusion that
lifts the work onto the level of great tragedy. The key of F minor was
used by Haydn from time to time for works of special intensity (one
recalls the F minor Symphony, No. 49, *La Passione*, or the string
quartet Op. 20 no. 5), and in a sense this work sums up his relationship
with this key. It is unusual for him to end a work in such unrelieved
darkness, and it shows clearly the strength and depth of Haydn's
emotional power. The man who wrote music such as this had an
understanding and compassion belonging only to the greatest artists.

Haydn's Piano Sonatas

John McCabe